re-discovering the

LOST AMERICAN PRINCIPLES

THE COUNTER-REVOLUTION

STEVEN L. HALL

Outskirts Press, Inc.
Denver, Colorado

The opinions expressed in this manuscript are solely the opinions of the author and do not represent the opinions or thoughts of the publisher. The author has represented and warranted full ownership and/or legal right to publish all the materials in this book.

Lost American Principles
the Counter-Revolution
All Rights Reserved.
Copyright © 2009 Steven L. Hall
V3.0

Cover Photo © 2009 JupiterImages Corporation. All rights reserved - used with permission.

This book may not be reproduced, transmitted, or stored in whole or in part by any means, including graphic, electronic, or mechanical without the express written consent of the publisher except in the case of brief quotations embodied in critical articles and reviews.

Outskirts Press, Inc.
http://www.outskirtspress.com

ISBN: 978-1-4327-4412-0

Library of Congress Control Number: 2009931496

Outskirts Press and the "OP" logo are trademarks belonging to Outskirts Press, Inc.
PRINTED IN THE UNITED STATES OF AMERICA

FPP!
S Hall

Dedication

To Patricia

To my kids and grandkids
To family and friends

and

To old friends re-discovered
(thank you, Malcolm)

Contents

Contents by Theme

Chapters:

Fundamental Principles and Goals 1-2
Natural rights and human nature 3-8
Discussions of Government 9-18
Guiding Principles for Governments 19
Discussions of Economics 20-31
Guiding Principles of Economics 32
America Today 33-34
The War Factor 35
A Look in the Mirror 36
Guiding Principles for Good Laws 37
Concluding thoughts 38
Constitutional Amendments .... Appendix A
Proposed new Political Party .... Appendix B

1. Big Trouble in River City 1
2. Where to Now? 3
3. Children 8
4. Right to Life, USA 10
5. Einstein and Wayne 13
6. you got no rights 21
7. Nature of Humans 28
8. The Need to Lead 33
9. Big, Bad Government 35
10. The Bully 40
11. Traffic Laws 42
12. Flawed Folks 44
13. Democracy 47
14. Four Dreams 51
15. A Living, Breathing Document 58
16. The Perfect Constitution 63
17. Freedom, but not Free 67
18. you got no rights II 71
19. Guiding Principles for Government 73
20. Close Encounter in the Woods 75
21. What's that in your pocket? *A chicken??* 78
22. The Coin Warehouse 81
23. Old Blue, the Ugly Horse 84
24. Smokey the Bear 87
25. Too Big to Fail 93
26. Toxic Assets 96
27. The Beach Boys (and girls): Endless Summer 101
28. What in the world is an "economist"? 104
29. Eat Your Vegetables 109
30. Going for the Gold 113
31. Real, Honest Money 117
32. Guiding Principles of Economics 120
33. Democracy versus Capitalism 123
34. The Great American Soap 127
35. Saved by the War 130
36. Mirror, Mirror 135
37. Guiding Principles for Good Laws 139
38. Solar: Energy of the Past 143
    Appendix A. Constitutional Amendments 146
    Appendix B. A new Political Party 151
    Chapter Notes and Resources 157
    Glossary of Terms 163
    Index 167

Chapter 1. Big Trouble in River City

Our economy is crumbling. Foreclosures, bankruptcies, bailouts, deficits, debt; these are the headlines - worldwide. Yet we seem to be doing more of the same things, faster, that landed us here. We have our military in two-thirds of the world's countries and are engaged in eternal wars. We have a myriad of issues facing us, from infrastructure to energy to climate change to education to . . .

We need to find solutions. Pretty darn quick. But not by arguing about tactics that stem from unsound theories in the first place; rather, we need to rebuild upon solid foundations. We need to re-discover the Idea of America. We must work together to identify the problems that we have brought upon ourselves, and correct them. And then find ways to resolve the challenges that are not our own fault, effectively.

> *This book is based on these Fundamental Principles:*

- that all people are created equal;
- that all people have certain natural Rights;
- that Government should be of the people, by the people, and for the people;
- and, that the Golden Rule is the most basic, most universal moral principle.

If you, too, believe in these principles, then we have a great deal of thinking to do, together.

This book started out as a series of letters to my kids and grandkids. Many of the topics herein are not discussed among friends or at family gatherings. Or in schools. That in itself is a sad commentary on the American condition. After all, democracy demands an understanding of governments and rights and freedoms and economies, as well as some means of choosing between alternative solutions to our problems. We need a foundation of principles that we can rely upon, that we can turn to when we must make important decisions. I submit that these

Lost American Principles: the Counter-revolution

can be found in the Idea of America, the Principles upon which the American experiment was originally based.

I have attempted to write in an easy-to-read, easy-to-understand style. Simple and straightforward. I may even be labeled "simplistic" by detractors, but simple truths are often, well . . . simple. That does not mean the solutions are easy; more often the gap between a simple realization like "I really need to quit smoking" and its actual accomplishment is filled with big challenges, self-discipline, hard choices, and pain.

The chapters are written so that most are self-contained, with a little story of its own to tell. So I apologize if some of the essential ideas are redundant. (But some bear repeating.)

A revolution is underway in America: slowly, quietly, the Idea of America is being dismantled. The American Principles are nearly lost. Whether we have enough democracy left, enough will, enough determination, enough grit, to put down this revolution remains to be seen.

We can only hope, and pray, that there *is* a counter-revolution, that the American Principles do not just fade away like a whipped pup sneaking off into the night, tail tucked between its legs. Because the ideals of Thomas Jefferson and George Washington and the other founders of the American experiment are worth fighting for.

It feels like there is indeed a counter-revolution mounting. It seems as though the two opposing forces are staging for a huge confrontation. It does not have to be bloody. Democracy can still prove itself worthy of our trust. Hanging in the balance is either the failure of this grand experiment, or another chance at its glory.

My wish for you, for your children, and for your grandchildren is simple: Freedom, Peace, and Prosperity. Here's to working together towards that end.

- - FPP - -

Chapter 2. Where to Now?

You have undoubtedly heard the saying, "If you don't know where you're going, you will probably wind up somewhere else." The importance of having goals, destinations, and objectives can hardly be overstated, especially when organizing people.

The questions are: what do we really want and expect of our governments? What do we want out of life? Most of the people I know just want to be left alone to live their lives in peace; to be healthy and safe; to enjoy their families; to learn and to express themselves; to have work and hobbies and pursuits that are rewarding; and to have the opportunity to succeed and create a better life for their children and grandchildren. Life, liberty and the pursuit of happiness. Freedom, Peace and Prosperity. That is all they expect or want from their governments.

<u>Freedom</u>

Freedom involves three parts: survival, and the defense of life; the liberty to do, say, and think as one pleases; and the freedom to own property. A society that desires Freedom would define these as "rights", meaning that each individual owns them and that no one can take them away. (Our founders called them "unalienable rights".)

When a society desires these rights for each of its citizens, then they can be formalized, usually with a written Constitution, to make them the law of the land, and thus create a Government to enforce that law. The function, then, the reason, the justification, and the role of Government, is the protection and defense of those Rights, insuring that one person's freedom does not infringe upon someone else's. And Government also has the responsibility not to use its *own* force to violate the rights of its individual citizens.

A person, or persons, empowered to use deadly force assume an awesome responsibility. When we entrust someone with money, we say they have a fiduciary responsibility, that they then have certain obligations. Similarly, when we entrust our Government with the use of deadly force, and with the power to arrest and imprison, they have an obligation to use their power very carefully.

It is important to note that a set of laws that guarantee individual Rights could be put into place by a benevolent King, a dictator, or even a totalitarian Government, if they chose to do so. The point is that Democracies do not necessarily produce Freedom; and even when they do, Democracies often let Freedom slip away. Remember this: <u>whether a country guards and defends the individual Rights of each of its citizens, then, is the real test of whether its people are Free.</u>

<u>Peace</u>

If Peace is one of our Goals, how will we know when we get there? Clearly we would not be at war; we would be getting along with our neighbors, the other countries in the world.

But how will that happen? By one country taking over the world and forcing peace upon it? By a coalition of countries using force to convert others to their way of thinking?

Or, in the end, will it happen when countries apply the Golden Rule? Individual citizens in free countries adhere to the standard that each may do as he or she pleases, as long as they do not infringe on someone else's right to do the same. (Refraining from doing to others what they would not want done to them.) Doesn't it seem reasonable that if countries were to follow that same simple principle, we would be much, much closer to achieving Peace?

Of course a country is entitled to a strong defense, capable of fending off every foreseeable threat. In fact, if the citizens of a country have a Right to Life, and thus to defend their lives, then a Government that would protect the rights of its citizens has an *obligation* to provide a strong national defense. Self-defense. But also, under the principle of the Golden Rule, Governments have the Responsibility to neither start wars, nor to meddle in the affairs of other countries, nor to do things to other countries that they would never tolerate having done to them.

If only we would understand and follow the advice of our first President, George Washington, when, before voluntar-

Where to now?

ily leaving office after two terms, he offered his best wishes to our young country in a series of letters. He said, "nothing is more essential than that permanent, inveterate antipathies against particular nations and passionate attachments for others, should be excluded." He encouraged and promoted free trade among nations, but warned us against playing favorites and forming permanent alliances; and, he cautioned us against defining certain nations as permanently hostile. Or evil.

The bottom line: nation building, bullying, meddling, and warring are the trademarks of Empires, and Empires always fall. A strong defense is not offensive; in fact, having the best military in the world is a fine and worthy goal, as long as the citizens fund that luxury, and as long as the military is used only for the defense of the citizens (defending their most basic Right, the Right to Life). And we must start asking the question: would we tolerate other countries doing, on our soil, what we are doing to them, in their lands? As long as the answer is to that question is "no", we will not attain peace.

Prosperity

When Prosperity is the Goal, how will we know when we have achieved it? I think we might agree that as a first measure of prosperity, we would know that every citizen has enough food, water, clothing, shelter, and basic health care to survive.

But beyond that, how would we define "prosperous"? Should every citizen be guaranteed a college education, a high paying job, a comfortable retirement, and unlimited health care? Should everyone have a home with a bedroom for each child, with a TV and a computer in every room? Should every family be guaranteed two cars in a three car garage? A garden? A swimming pool? Very hard to draw the line, yes? Perhaps we should think about where "prosperity" comes from.

In many countries, even today, if the people were able to provide the basics *for themselves*, they would consider themselves prosperous. That is, if they could produce their own food, water, clothing, shelter, and health care, without outside help or assistance, they would not want for much more. At least not for a while.

So how do people move from poverty to that first level of prosperity, to self-reliance? It's pretty simple, really. They have to be set free to do what humans do. They need to have private property so that they can use it to produce, grow food, find materials, and make products. And then trade, creating markets. It happens very quickly when individual Rights are acknowledged and protected, especially private property rights. Oh sure, they might need an initial helping hand. But in virtually every country where the people are in poverty, you will find that their Government either denies them private property rights, restricts and controls free markets, or confiscates their property.

We Americans long ago reached that first level of prosperity and have gone well beyond. Where does the additional prosperity come from? It comes from individuals producing goods and services, and then trading them for things they want more. It comes from saving more than one consumes, which creates capital, and then using that capital to buy tools that increase productivity even more. And then trading. Making a profit. Saving some. Investing again. And so on . . .

This process increases the wealth of the entire country, although never evenly or all at once, of course. But because it frees humans to do what they do naturally, it is by far the best way to achieve prosperity. Any system that inhibits humans from doing what they naturally do, forces them to act *un*naturally, restricts their individual freedom, will simultaneously reduce their productivity. And ultimately limits the prosperity of the country.

So the answer to the how-much-prosperity puzzle is that once that first level of prosperity is reached, once the citizens are self-sufficient and able to provide the basics for themselves, then the rest is simply up to them. If they are free, then they can choose to produce as little or as much as they wish to, and as much as they are able to. Governments simply cannot force people to prosper. Bringing Government force into the marketplace only makes things harder over the long run; in fact, Gov-

Where to now?

ernment attempts to operate or control markets generally result in making real prosperity impossible.

FPP

"FPP" stands for Freedom, Peace, and Prosperity. What more could we ask of our Government? What more could we want?
    In the final analysis, Freedom is simply the recognition of, and protection of, individual Rights. It is that Freedom that produces prosperity. And Freedom provides the framework for internal Peace within a country (never fully achieved, of course, because not all people are good all the time).
    The framework for external Peace, between countries, will only occur when we apply the same principles.

FPP is the goal, the direction, the challenge. Like many lofty goals, we may never fully achieve it, and certainly not in our lifetimes. But it is worth the effort, for our children and for our grandchildren - and it will make for an exciting journey.

- FPP -

Chapter 3. Children

"Listen to my new song." . . . "Will you come to our play?"

"I'll race you to that tree." . . . "Can I join your club?"

"That's *mine*! Mom, he took it! It's mine!" . . . "I'll trade you one of these for two of those."

"My favorite color is blue." . . . "My dog is smarter than yours."

All kids do these things. It's their nature. It's human nature. To suppress, or deny, these acts is to suppress human nature. Yes, kids think and dream, too, experience fear and love, have all of their thoughts and emotions. Some of which we may never know. But these are the *actions* of all kids.

Why would we keep children from communicating, reading, writing, speaking, learning, expressing themselves, singing, dancing, painting, performing a play?
     Why we would prevent kids from competing, from playing games? And from joining together for common interests, clubs, teams, church groups, activities?
     Why would we not allow them ownership of their own "stuff"? And allow them to trade some of their stuff for something they want more?
     Why would we discourage them from prioritizing, from distinguishing bad, good, better, best; from establishing goals for themselves?

The only justification, it seems apparent, for not allowing these acts is when the kid hurts someone else by doing so. Kids have a right, a *need*, to communicate; to compete/join; to own/trade; and to prioritize.
     In the end, we are all kids in that regard. We adults have the same needs; it's our nature. That's how we grow. When these actions are denied or prohibited, we simply stop growing as humans; we shrivel, become less free, less happy, less prosperous, and less . . . human.

Children

The lesson is pretty simple: because we are human, we have a right to be human. And because these acts are human nature, natural, we have a right to communicate; a right to compete and to join; a right to own and to trade; and, a right to prioritize, for ourselves.

These rights, of course, stem from the first right, the right for kids to live in the first place. And to stay alive.

When you want to understand natural human rights, just watch the children.

- FPP -

Chapter 4. Right to Life, USA

I am a judge, driving to a far corner of the State. As I enter a small town, the sign reads, "Welcome to our City, Right to Life, USA." Followed by, "No abortions in the last 22 years." The number twenty-two is obviously hand-written; clearly they are proud of the fact. I need to find out why, and how . . .

As I cruise through town, something seems strange, unnatural. I pass an empty park, with deserted play fields, and it finally dawns - - there are no children. It is after school, but before dinner time, and it is a clear day. I see one youngster playing in a yard, but it is odd not to have children running about everywhere.

Then I am at the hospital, witnessing a birth. The baby, a chubby, healthy boy, is wiped down and wrapped in a towel. But rather than hand him to his mother, the attendants rush him out the door. Curious, I follow. In another room, they enter the baby's exact time of birth onto a page in a large Journal, along with his weight and length, the color of his eyes and hair, and his mother's information. Then they stamp an imprint of his right hand and his right foot into the journal. And the person in charge signs at the bottom of the page.

I follow them through another door that takes us outside. They place the baby in a basket, wrapped only in the towel, and they put the basket in the center of the plaza in the town square. And then they leave. The baby cries and screams. People on the sidewalks hear the screams and bow their heads as if to pray, or make the sign of the cross. But no one enters the plaza. I cry too, bewildered.

"We believe that the Right to Life is the most fundamental right, the most precious gift, that God has given each of us," the Authority was explaining to me, "and we have abolished abortion in our City, for over 20 years now."

"The sign says 22 years," I reply, "but why did you put the baby in a basket, why are you not feeding him or protecting him?"

The Authority says, "He is in God's hands now. We have protected and defended his Right to Life; we have logged him into the Journal. If it is God's will that he survive for six days, then on the seventh day we will stamp the prints of his left hand and foot into the Journal, and return him to his mother."

I am dumfounded. The right to life, but not the right to continue to live? That explains the lack of children in Right to Life. And why there are few birthdays celebrated in the winter months.

A few blocks behind the hospital, I encounter homeless people, ragged and obviously starving, living in pallor, rummaging through the garbage, their children begging for handouts.

The Authority says, "They are in God's hands. It is His will. They are free to find work and earn their way if they so choose. Besides, if we were to give them new clothes and a home, or worse, if we were to enable them to provide for themselves, we would deny our congregation the opportunity to be charitable, and to gain favor in the eyes of God."

Again, the right to life, but not the right to live.

On another street, I find a man in a jail - - more like a cage - - shivering and wasting away. He tells me that he is condemned to die.

"But doesn't God say thou shalt not kill?" I ask the Authority. "You say that you believe in the Right to Life, but does that not include the Right to Live? Aren't you denying this man an opportunity to reconcile with God? To seek His forgiveness? Killing in self-defense is one thing, but this man is in a cage. He may not be innocent, but he is helpless. Did Jesus not preach forgiveness in place of revenge? What if that man, as so many have been, is wrongly convicted and is actually innocent? What if God has plans for him, maybe even a plan to forgive him? Will God forgive *us* for taking his life?"

The Authority has heard it all before and rolls his eyes.

I am red in the face with frustration, sweating. I shudder. How can the people of Right to Life be so committed to bringing children into the world and yet not be equally committed to their Right to Live? If we have a Right to Life, do we not also have a right to the basic food, water, clothing, shelter and health

Lost American Principles: the Counter-revolution

care needed to sustain life? As well as a responsibility to refrain from exterminating people in cages?

And then I think of the people who *do* recognize our obligation to provide the basic means of life, to ensure that our neighbors can survive. And who are against capital punishment. In other words, they are committed to the Right to Live.

And yet, ironically, they crusade against the Right to Life for those who are living but are yet unborn.

I awaken from the nightmare, relieved that I am not a judge.

- FPP -

Chapter 5. Einstein and Wayne

Living in Alaska allows one an incredible interaction with nature; the sheer magnitude and power is awe-inspiring. Merely surviving is often a challenge. The constant, ever-changing tension between nature and man - - which will prevail? - - is in many ways the same battle that humans wage individually: "Can my rational mind, and my heart and soul, prevail over my baser nature?"

And the folks who live in Alaska are a varied and colorful lot. Some come to escape, others to explore. Some come to experience nature's beauty, others to try to express their own. Adventurers, artists, and rogues. Cynics and poets. The industrious and the paranoid. And a few of them seem to be all of those things at once.

I sometimes wander down the Yukon Bar to sip on a Moose Tooth IPA beer, just to sit at the bar and people-watch. One day I noticed a couple of men, apparently Alaskans, sitting and talking. They seemed an odd pair. The first was small and slim, wearing an old tattered jacket and a faded, wool cap with furry flaps pulled down over his ears. When he spoke, I could see, from clear across the bar, that he was missing several teeth.

The second man had a large frame, and was wearing a clean, plaid wool shirt. He had snow-white hair, his red-streaked beard neatly trimmed. His hands were large and calloused; he looked like a combination of John Wayne and Paul Bunyan. (That is, John and Paul in their retirement years.) I could not hear what they were saying from where I sat.

On my next visit, I took up the stool nearest to where they were again sitting and talking. My back was to them, but I could sometimes hear a few words over the noise of the jukebox and the televisions. When I heard, "and God encouraged slavery," my curiosity was aroused. I asked the bartender, "Who are those guys sitting behind me?"

"Oh," he chuckled, "That's Einstein and Wayne. The Philosopher and his sidekick. One thinks he is inspired and the other one is a few cards short of a full deck. Like the Lone Ranger and Tonto," he went on, "did you know that "tonto" means idiot, or fool, in Spanish?" He seemed eager to fill me in; he obviously felt that they were both pretty weird, even by Alaskan standards.

I asked which was which. "Einstein is the little one," he replied.

"Do you think they would mind if I joined them?" I asked, possessed by a sudden urge to join the conversation.

"It's a free country," the bartender said, as he shrugged his shoulders and shot me one of those "what-is-wrong-with-you?" looks. He no longer wanted to talk to me . . .

Keystone Light might be the most popular beer in Alaska. It is certainly among the most affordable and most available, even in the bush. That's what Einstein and Wayne drank. I ordered two cans. As I approached, asking if I might join them, Einstein's bright eyes lit up; he looked at me, then at the beers, and gave me a warm, ear-to-ear, infectious grin. "Sure," he said, offering a handshake, "sit down". The lumberjack turned his head, sized me up, and turned back, without a word.

In Alaska, Winter releases her icy grip slowly, teasing us with sunny days followed by freezing nights. For weeks. And just when you think it is over, she dumps more snow. But this was one of those early Spring days, clear and sunny, not a cloud in the sky, and it had warmed all the way up to forty-six degrees. To us it felt like seventy. People shed their jackets and put on shorts. And Einstein had left his wool cap at home.

Without his hat, Einstein looked like every picture of Albert Einstein that I remember seeing. Well, maybe Albert had all of his teeth, but this Einstein's grey hair was sticking out in every direction, as if he had been hit by a bolt of lightning. He took both cans of Keystone Light from me, handed one to Wayne, and their conversation resumed as if I was not there.

I never recorded these meetings, but I always scribbled notes after. So I will do my best to retell them accurately. I am probably paraphrasing and consolidating; and I apologize in advance to Einstein and Wayne if I misrepresent anything they said.

I probably sat down with these two crusty, colorful Alaskans on four or five occasions; they constantly challenged my beliefs. It turned out they were both widowers; they lived together in a little cabin out of convenience. Einstein said he was 74 years old. Wayne said he was 70, but I suspect he was rounding down. It was but a few minutes into our first meeting that I realized that Einstein was the sidekick - - nicknamed for his hair rather than his brains - - and that the big guy, Wayne, was actually the "philosopher". Looks don't give us much insight into people, do they?

Wayne was very deliberate when he "taught" Einstein; he sometimes struggled to put a lofty concept into words. Einstein would try his best to concentrate, to understand. Sometimes he seemed to "get it". But he was just as likely to blurt out something completely contradictory. When he got mentally sidetracked, which was often, he would grin at me and raise his beer. That usually meant that it was time for me to buy another round. Wayne would pause, ignoring the commotion and the interruptions, and then pick up right where he left off.

I rarely offered my own opinions. Nor did I want to. These two were allowing me to sit in on their fascinating dialogue. Occasionally, though, I would ask a question. Here are pieces and bits of some of the conversations, as best I recall them:

- - - -

Wayne said, "Leonard," [note: "Einstein's" real name, I learned, was Leonard; Wayne only called him by his nickname "Einstein" when he was frustrated with him] "Leonard, God didn't make man in His own image; men made God in their image. And it was men doing the making. Why else would God be a man? Wouldn't you think God would be a woman?"

Leonard looked puzzled, "But He is the King of kings, right?"

Wayne continued, "A female God would be loving and nurturing and protecting and cultivating, like a woman tending her garden. The God men made is an old man who sits on a throne and makes rash decisions and throws lightning bolts whenever He is upset, which is nearly all of the time."

- - - -

Another time, Wayne was commenting, as he often did, on one of the stories from the Old Testament, "So where did we get the idea of only one wife in a marriage, Leonard? In One Kings, Solomon had seven hundred wives and three hundred concubines. To get to each one even once a year, he would have to be with about three a day. Do you think maybe he just used them once?" Leonard looked a little dazed, trying to picture hundreds of available women.

- - - -

Leonard had asked Wayne if things wouldn't be better if we just followed the Ten Commandments (perhaps he had been listening to talk radio that morning). "OK, Einstein, *which* ten commandments?" Wayne asked him impatiently.

"Well, *the* Ten Commandments", Leonard responded quizzically. Leonard believed the Bible to be Word of God.

Wayne said, "In Exodus 34:28, God brought Moses up to Mount Sinai and gave him the laws that the Bible calls the ten commandments, written in stone, to replace the ones that got busted. But these laws were not the ones we hear today, these ten commandments were about destroying altars, not worshipping the other gods, and the proper procedures and recipes for killing birds and animals for sacrifice."

Leonard was trying to follow. "Do you mean there are two different ten commandments?"

Wayne said, "Yes, the ones that Charlton Heston brought down the hill in the movies were not called the ten commandments in the Bible. But those are the ones you see printed everywhere. And the last half of those are just common-sense rules for any society. The first half are about how to worship the God of the tribes. The Golden Rule could replace all of them and would apply to people of every religion."

- - - -

One day, I could not resist the temptation to jump in. "What about government?" I asked.

Einstein and Wayne

Wayne's eyes appeared jet black as he stared right into me. After a few unblinking moments, he said, "You don't mess with me. And I won't mess with you. That's all the government I need. That's all the government anyone needs." And then he resumed his dialogue with Leonard.

I knew in that moment that I would never "mess" with Wayne. And I suspect that no one does, unless they are itching for some punishment. He did not have to threaten or pull a weapon. His frame was large and strong, yes, but it was also his body language, his matter-of-fact approach, his resolve, his rationality . . . his calm way of delivering the message. I did not fear him, because I also sensed that he would not "mess" with me, either. But I knew - - and it appeared that everyone else did as well - - that Wayne was not a person whose rights could be easily violated.

- - - -

"The Word of God? *The Word of God?* OK, Einstein, who *wrote* the Bible?" Wayne was obviously more than a little worked up and frustrated with Leonard, who had kind of curled up on his barstool, feet on the seat, back to the wall, as if to turn away from this confrontation. I went and ordered a couple more Keystone Lights.

When I got back with the beers, Wayne was talking faster and louder than usual, "The Bible was written by *men*, by humans, in Hebrew and Aramic and Greek and then Latin and then English. They didn't have printing presses, so they wrote the stories by hand, over and over. Have you ever played the game where one person whispers a story into another person's ear, and then they repeat it around a circle? It's always different and distorted by the end. Same with these stories. And then other men interpreted and edited, allowed some stuff to be put in and decided other stuff should be left out. The Bible is just the stories passed down from a wandering tribe who happened to be infatuated with keeping records."

Lost American Principles: the Counter-revolution

Wayne took a deep breath and paused after that little outburst. He downed half a beer and then continued in his calmer, more deliberate tone. "The Bible is the diary of a tribe of people who were competing with other tribes. They fought over everything. They fought about who had the best gods. They were like the Ken-L Ration commercial, "my god's better than your god." It is very hard to tell which tribes won what, probably nobody won in the end, but the so-called "chosen people" kept the best written accounts of how they went from believing in many powerful gods to eventually thinking their God was the best."

- - - -

On another occasion, Wayne returned to his "men made God in their own image" theme. He said, "Why else would God be a King? Why would God get so enraged with his own creations? Why is He so jealous and bitter and humorless and merciless? Those are the personalities of man. Why does He rule through fear? Why does He practice favoritism? Why all the vengeance and wrath? Is He really such an unhappy, maladjusted God? No sense of humor? Why does He deal in slavery and death? Why does He smite - - or have his "people" kill - - hundreds of thousands of innocent people, even their own relatives and children? Why all of the bloody sacrifices? One answer Leonard: because these are the acts of men, and men created God in their own image. They had to justify their superstitions and their unholy impulses and their cruel behaviors somehow."

During these little "get-togethers", Wayne often referred to Bible chapters or verses that illustrated his points. Numbers 25 where Phineas sees a mixed-race couple and spears them to death, because of their race. Exodus where God does battle with the other gods at enormous costs in innocent lives. The instructions for animal sacrifices in Leviticus, or Noah's first act after landfall, sacrificing some of the animals he had just saved. Judges 11 where God asks a man to sacrifice his innocent daughter, and he does. Samuel 24 where 70,000 Israelites are slain. Wayne had obviously read the entire Bible, apparently many times, and had his mind made up about these things.

And he had some very convincing arguments. But I wanted to read for myself some of those passages, to study and think about these things, to bring back some ammunition to confront him with, because my entire upbringing and understanding were quite at odds with nearly everything he told Leonard.

- - - -

One day, Leonard finally asked Wayne the question that I had been wanting to ask myself, "So Wayne, do you believe in God or not?"

Wayne leaned forward and said, "Of course I do. But God is not something outside of us, Leonard; God is not a *person*. God is something we cannot fully understand. Leonard, think of this: think of a caterpillar crawling slowly up a branch. And then a butterfly lands on the branch in front of him. Do you think the caterpillar even knows what the butterfly is? Or that is what he is destined to become?"

It took Leonard a minute. "No, I suppose not," he said.

Wayne said, "Well I do not think we can comprehend God, either, because God is a force beyond our understanding. But I think that force can enter into us if we allow it, sort of like water coming into a plant. Or, we can block that God-force, we can choose to keep God away from us and out of our lives, because we have free will and free choice. Anyway, that's how I see it."

- - - -

April melted into May, and Spring had arrived in Seward for real. The snow crept out of the valleys and rolled itself up the mountainsides, revealing the bounty underneath. The bears were shaking off their long sleep and were ravenous. Birds and buds were popping out everywhere.

I could hardly wait to get down to the Yukon Bar and sit down with my friends. (Well, I may be exaggerating that we were friends; I bought them beer and they tolerated me.) But they were not there. I asked the bartender, "Where's Einstein and Wayne?"

"Hell, I don't know," he said, "this is usually the time of year they head out for the summer. They might go down to Homer or Anchor Point, maybe Cordova. Maybe Fairbanks.

They been all over. Sometimes they come back here for the winter, sometimes no. Nobody knows with them two."

It didn't register for a minute. Then I realized that they were gone.

"Thank them. God bless them," I said. The bartender moved away from me, wiping down the bar as he went. He shot me a sideways glance that said "what-an-idiot". I didn't care.

Outside the bar, the steep mountains reflected across Resurrection Bay, deep green forests greeting snowy glaciers. I inhaled the pungent salt air and listened to the gulls chattering and arguing. Fishing boats headed out of the harbor, filled with anticipation. I felt alive.

I would miss our "Godversations", and think about them often. Most of what Wayne said was at odds with what I had been taught, contradicted the teachings of my church. Leonard was unconvinced, too. But I guess it made me realize, in a way I never had before, the importance of freedom of religion. Wayne had every right to his beliefs. And I had no right to say he could *not* believe as he did, or to impose some set of religious values upon him, as long as he was civil, as long as he did not force his beliefs on me, either. As long as he did not hurt anyone else - and I really do not think he ever would.

- FPP -

Chapter 6. you got no rights

The late, great comedian George Carlin said, "There's no such thing as rights." And he did a comedy bit based on the proposition that we have no rights.

Yet our country, and our Government, sprung from the idea that all of us are equal and thus have unalienable rights. We started this book off with that simple premise. In fact, it is the most fundamental idea not only of this book, but also of most nations that consider themselves free.

What *are* "rights"? The word is used so often, and often so loosely, that it is hard to determine what is meant. So I did the modern thing, a computer search. Which turned up a couple of definitions:

One website assigned the attributes of rights as something like just, proper, and fitting.

Another definition included the idea of having rights protected by the government under a contract.

Those were helpful, although a little generic in terms of seeking to understand the nature of rights. So I clicked on a link that took me to the *Stanford Encyclopedia of Philosophy,** where I found a thorough examination of rights:

"The four basic . . . "elements" [of rights] are the privilege, the claim, the power, and the immunity." The article differentiates between active and passive rights, and between positive and negative rights. It talks about the Will Theory and the Interest Theory. And Conceptual Analysis versus Definitional Stipulation.

[*footnote: Wenar, Leif, "Rights", *The Stanford Encyclopedia of Philosophy (Fall 2008 Edition)*, Edward N. Zalta (ed.), URL = http://plato.stanford.edu/archives/fall2008/entries/rights/]

As I tried to follow all of this, I said to myself, aloud, "whoa" . . . whoosh - right over my head. But then the article moved on to some points that were, for me, more understandable. It talks about "status-based rights", which "belong to the tradition" of natural rights:

"All natural rights theories fix upon features that humans have by their nature, and which make respect for certain rights appropriate." Non-religious theories, it points out, often align with theories based on morals, and contain these attributes: "rationality, free will, autonomy, the ability to regulate one's life in accordance with one's chosen conception of the good life."

The article points out that it was this theory, promoted by Hobbes and Locke and others, that influenced Thomas Jefferson when he wrote "We hold these truths to be self-evident, that all men are created equal, that they are endowed by their Creator with certain unalienable rights, that among these are Life, Liberty, and the Pursuit of Happiness."

It said that Nozick revived the theory within the philosophy community when he wrote, ""Individuals have rights," he wrote, "and there are things no person or group may do to them (without violating their rights)" (Nozick 1974, ix).

It goes on to say, "Many find this grounding of rights in individual dignity appealing. There is also a directness and clarity to status explanations of fundamental rights . . . Moreover, status-based rights are attractively robust. While the justifications of instrumental rights are always contingent on calculations concerning consequences, status-based rights are anchored firmly in individual dignity. This makes it easy to explain why status-based rights are strong, almost unqualified rights, and this is a position which many believe properly expresses the great value of each individual."

OK, so that is what I believe. Like Locke and Jefferson and the natural rights philosophers, I believe that each of us has unalienable rights. Regardless of whether these rights come from God or from simply being human. That belief matches up with one of the definition of rights that I found on the web: just, proper, and fitting. The challenge, of course, is how best to accomplish the other description, to make those rights "legal"; that is, protected by the government.

    Ah, but that's not the end of the story. Because not everyone agrees. (Surprised?) *Stanford Encyclopedia of Philosophy* goes on to say that some propose "instrumental rights" and "egalitarian rights", which basically argue that rights are only justified when they serve the greater good, although these folks disagree on what constitutes, and how to measure, "the greater good". Therein lies the problem: who then *decides* what rights we have? Because, if this route is pursued, then George Carlin was correct when he asserted that we really have no rights: "Rights aren't rights if someone can take 'em away," he said, "they're privileges . . . temporary privileges!" Privileges that the Government can grant - or take away.

The final chapter in the *Stanford Encyclopedia of Philosophy* article about rights is called "Critiques of Rights" and it turns to Carl Marx, perhaps the best known and the most critical. It is important to understand his views, because many of his arguments are widely employed today. The website says:

    "Marx attacked the substance of the revolutionary eighteenth century American and French political documents that proclaimed the fundamental "rights of man": liberty, equality, security, property, and the free exercise of religion. Marx objected that these alleged rights derive from a false conception of the human individual as unrelated to others, as having interests that can be defined without reference to others, and as always potentially in conflict with others. The rights-bearing individual is an "isolated nomad…withdrawn behind his private interests and whims and separated from the community." (Marx 1844, 146).

    "The right of property, Marx asserted, exemplifies the isolating and anti-social character of these alleged rights of man. On the one hand, the right of property is the right to keep others at a distance: the legal equivalent of a barbed wire fence. On the other hand, the right of property allows an owner to transfer his resources at his own pleasure and for his own gain, without regard even for the desperate need for those resources elsewhere."

"Similarly, Marx held that the much-celebrated individual right to liberty is based upon and reinforces selfishness. Those who are ascribed the right to do what they wish so long as they do not hurt others will perpetuate a culture of egoistical obsession. As for equality, the achievement of equal rights merely distracts people from noticing that their equality is purely formal: a society with formally equal rights will continue to be divided by huge inequalities in economic and political power. *Finally, these so-called "natural" rights are in fact not natural to humans at all. They are simply the defining elements of the rules of the modern mode of production, perfectly suited to fit each individual into the capitalist machine.*"

I added the italics to the last sentence. But please re-read and think about those last three paragraphs. Marx denies all individual rights, including liberty, equality, security, property, and freedom of religion. Marx argued that private property rights isolated people rather than meeting the needs of the greater society. That liberty leads to selfishness. And that natural rights are nothing more than a creation of the capitalist machine, designed to enslave people.

It is ironic that in spite of the failures of socialism around the world, and although we Americans have fought an enormous war of ideals against communism, we are still embracing many of Marx's theories. The anti-communist movement has been replaced by an anti-capitalist movement. You can hardly go a day without hearing about the weaknesses and flaws in free markets, or the evils of capitalism.

Nobel Prize winning economist Milton Friedman said, "Today, there is wide agreement that socialism is a failure, capitalism a success. Yet . . . the bulk of the intellectual community almost automatically favors any expansion of government power so long as it is advertised as a way to protect individuals from big bad corporations, relieve poverty, protect the environment, or promote "equality"."

Look at the implications of Marx theories: people are not equal and each must be treated differently, as the Government determines best; free speech must be suppressed and the Government shall decide what can be written, spoken, read, or heard; all property belongs to the Government; the Government will define what people need, where they should live, and what their work will be; and the Government will decide what religions will be allowed. Marx wrote of ten conditions to accomplish the transition from capitalism to communism:

1. Abolition of private property and the application of all rents of land to public purposes.

2. A heavy progressive or graduated income tax.

3. Abolition of all rights of inheritance.

4. Confiscation of the property of all emigrants and rebels.

5. Centralization of credit in the hands of the state, by means of a national bank with State capital and an exclusive monopoly.

6. Centralization of the means of communications and transportation in the hands of the State.

7. Extension of factories and instruments of production owned by the state, the bringing into cultivation of waste lands, and the improvement of the soil generally in accordance with a common plan.

8. Equal liability of all to labor. Establishment of industrial armies, especially for agriculture.

9. Combination of agriculture with manufacturing industries, gradual abolition of the distinction between town and country, by a more equitable distribution of population over the country.

10. Free education for all children in public schools. Abolition of children's factory labor in its present form. Combination of education with industrial production.

So, if we are so opposed to communism, how have we managed to adopt, or move toward, most of the planks of the communist party, the steps Marx thought necessary to change a capitalist

Lost American Principles: the Counter-revolution

country to communist? Are there some of these that could actually exist in a truly free country, or are they all extensions of Marx premise that we do not have individual rights?

Look – let's be fair. Marx also said that once people were basically (forced to be) happy under this system, that the Government would wither away and disappear. So all of these so-called "violations" of our liberty serve only to make society better; they are done for our own good. But ask the questions: Do the ends justify the means? And - does a tyrannical, authoritarian Government ever "wither away"?

Perhaps this is the most important question: was Marx correct that natural human rights are just a creation of the capitalists? A plot to enslave the people? That our so-called individual rights and liberties actually *violate* human nature?

Therein is the heart of the argument. In the next chapter we will talk about the nature of humans. And I trust that we will find that natural rights are an extension of human nature, and that protecting those rights, as a by-product, also maximizes the well-being of the greater society.

In the end, I believe that Marx's theories simply propose to suppress and control human nature, by deadly force whenever necessary, in order to achieve some ideal. (In fact, it appears that Marx wanted to achieve peace and prosperity in a society, just as we do.) But the fatal flaw of socialism is that the use of deadly force to restrict individual liberty, regardless of the "higher purpose", can only restrict human nature, limit what we humans do. And because it so violates human nature, it takes ever more and stricter Government to sustain it.

The net result of socialism is poverty. Economic poverty, of course. But also a poverty of ideas and creativity; a lack of self-reliance and personal responsibility; a shortage of real charity; and a deficiency of self-worth and hope.

Marx was wrong. Individuals are important. Each one. We come "built-in" with certain natural rights, rights to freely express our human nature and to grow. You must decide whether you believe the same. Or whether in your heart you feel that the needs of the greater society are more important than any individual; and that "rights" are just an illusion promoted by the capitalists to serve their own ends; that there are not rights, there are only the permissions that our Government chooses to grant us.

We will proceed on the assumption that many of us still believe in the ideals upon which our Constitution was founded. And that each of us really does have a right to life, to liberty, and to the pursuit of happiness.

Remember George Carlin's admonition, "Rights aren't rights if someone can take 'em away." So how do we establish a society where rights are protected by law, *cannot* be taken away? We need a Government that is itself subject to a higher law, the Rule of Law, where little "r" rights are protected by the law of the land. Then we can call them big "R" Rights.

- FPP -

Chapter 7. Nature of Humans

So the essence of Carl Marx's theories is that individual humans are neither important nor are they entitled to rights. That societies of people are like beehives or anthills, it is only the "success" of the swarm or the colony that is important. (You might want to watch the movie "Antz" again.)

I don't buy it. It seems like Marx started with the idea that he hated capitalism, for whatever reasons, and then invented a twisted theory of human nature that would justify the idea of a government without capitalism. (Rather than first looking at human nature, and from there developing a theory of government.) In other words, to reach his goal of government sans capitalists, he had to argue against human nature. And human rights.

But we disagree with Marx, so we are assuming the existence of certain unalienable rights, including the freedom to believe, or not believe, in whatever religion(s) we choose.

So what is the nature of us humans? First off, let's not get into the argument about whether humans are created by God, or by which God, or whether we are mammals descended from lower life forms. Because I do not pretend to be in any position to tell you what to believe. More importantly, if we are to have Freedom of Religion, *nobody* ought to be in a position to tell you what you must believe. And if you want to preserve your right to your own beliefs, then you must also support the rights of others to theirs, to believe differently.

Let's be practical. Instead to engaging in esoteric inquiries into what humans *are*, let's explore what it is that humans *do*. After all, we know that we think and dream; love and hate; imagine and plan; plot and scheme; and experience sorrow, fear, and joy. We humans experience an enormous range of imaginations, thoughts, urges, and emotions. Yet, even with extensive observation and analysis, even with the most modern technologies and techniques, the truth is simply this:
we can never know, for certain, what another person is truly thinking or feeling.* We must, then, work within the framework of what we can observe and know: human actions.

Nature of Humans

Here are some basic things that humans do, by nature; that is to say, *naturally:*

1. Survive
2. Communicate
3. Compete
4. Trade
5. Prioritize

These are human nature, these are human inclinations, these are what we do when we are being . . . human. It seems that if we were created that way, whether by God or by nature or by cosmic forces, that we ought to be free to act accordingly. We have a need to be able, voluntarily, to perform these acts, or to choose not to. Constrained, of course, if everyone is to have the same rights, by the Golden Rule.

"Now wait a minute", you say, "humans also rob, cheat, steal, and kill. Does that mean they have a right to do those things too?" No. Not only because we may find such acts morally wrong, but more importantly because they violate someone else's rights. ("Moral", by the way, can be a dangerous standard, because there are always those who will argue that in certain cases objectionable acts become "morally" justifiable.)

What we are saying is that each of these human tendencies to act, these things that humans do, implies a right to do them - as long as we are not hurting someone else by doing so.

[*footnote: It is worth pointing out - - if you do believe in God - - that you can never know for sure what another person's relationship with God is, either, what the two of them are thinking or feeling towards one another. Or if that relationship is about to change. That has serious policy implications, particularly if you would interfere with God's plan or relationships.]

Lost American Principles: the Counter-revolution

So let's look at each of these, and think about the rights that follow:

1. <u>Survival</u> is the most basic instinct in nature. Animals, when their lives are threatened, are very dangerous and unpredictable; they will do things they would otherwise never do. Humans are the same in that regard. If we are to have a safe and somewhat predictable society, then we must ensure survival.

The right to Life is the most fundamental right, the one that anchors everything else we do. After all, if we do not have a right to live, if someone else has the right or authority to take our life, of what possible benefit are the rest of our rights?

The right to Life implies the right to defend one's life. Self-defense. And defines the responsibility of not taking the life of another.

But the right to Life also implies the right to Survive. That is, it's not enough that we can defend against someone taking our life, it follows that we must also have the right to *continue* to live; and for that we need food, potable water, clothing, shelter, and basic health care. These are not only the rights of each human being, but they also then become the simultaneous responsibilities of every person as well.

2. We <u>communicate</u>. But human communication hardly ends with making speeches and writing books. We communicate through body language, through dress, through dance. We communicate through paintings and art. We communicate through music. Freedom of expression is essential to the pursuit of happiness.

So we have the right to freely communicate and express ourselves. Or to choose not to express ourselves in one manner or another. Thus another person, having the same rights, must then be free to choose not to listen, not to read, not to watch, not to dance . . . not to receive our communication, if she so chooses.

The right to communicate is defined by some of its aspects, Freedom of Speech and Freedom of the Press, for example. I probably do not need to expound on these, most of us know that they are essential to freedom.

Nature of Humans

The hard part is realizing and defending everyone else's same right to communicate, even those with whom we disagree. And then balancing one person's right to communicate against the right of the next person to choose *not* to receive that communication.

3. We compete. From the time we are children: "Race you!" And throughout our lives, we compete for mates, for jobs, for positions of leadership, for, well . . . almost everything. In games, sports, politics, economics, everywhere. It is natural. So we can infer that we have a right to compete.

The word "compete" is often used in that way: "to strive . . . for an objective" or "to be in a state of rivalry".* Competition is in fact sometimes viewed negatively, as if it should not be part of human nature, as if we could somehow deny it. The real problem is in how we structure "competitions" and how we perceive the results; the tendencies to pursue goals and to engage in competition are not bad things.

But that is only one way to look at the word "compete". Look at the origin of the word: it comes from the Latin "*competere*" . . . "to seek together" . . . "to come together".* Yes, we strive for goals and objectives, and often as rivals. But perhaps even more importantly, when we "compete", we can also *come together* and *join* forces to accomplish common goals and objectives. We form clubs, teams, associations, groups, partnerships, corporations . . . and we instinctively know that we can accomplish more when we work together.

The Right to Join (voluntarily) is an extension of the Right to Compete (to strive for our goals).

[*footnote: By permission. From the *Merriam-Webster Online Dictionary*©2009 by Merriam-Webster, Incorporated
www.Merriam-Webster.com]

Lost American Principles: the Counter-revolution

4. We trade. People naturally own stuff. Watch any two year old saying, "that's mine". Private Property Rights are generally recognized as unalienable human rights. (Except, of course, by socialists, communists, tyrants, and kings.)

But equally as important is The Right to Trade. That is, to trade my stuff for your stuff, when I want to and when you want to. This is the essence of economic freedom. After all, the two alternatives are poor ones: that we are forced to trade our stuff against our will; or, that we are prevented from trading even when we want to.

5. And we prioritize. We naturally, constantly make individual decisions about what is most important for us, at any given time. Stranded in a hot desert, a drink of water may be the highest priority in one's life; but on a normal day in the suburbs, maybe not so much. We rank things, order things, categorize. We score and weigh and balance. We set goals and execute strategies - - we live our lives - - based on our priorities, which are, for each of us, actually a constant stream of ever-changing preferences.

Having a right to our own priorities is simply the Right to Free Choice.

- FPP -

Chapter 8. The Need to Lead

What is it about some people that they have a need to control others? Why do some seek humbly to contribute, and thus make a commitment to lead, while others seem *driven* to control, to command, to be the ruler? Is it a craving for power? Are they vain? Are they without doubt? Convinced that they know how to control the world?

We all know people like this. Would-be kings probably *require* all of those traits. After all, if one is to be the supreme ruler, to make the laws for all, to control life and death and destinies, then one probably has to be convinced that he is, in fact, God on earth. For that is what kings do, play God. As do tyrants and dictators and authoritarians. It's a top-down hierarchy that feeds the ego, and all of the desires, of the King, while everyone else receives whatever the King sees fit to "bless" them with.

There are far too many among us who have the need to lead. Too many who lust for the power over others, or the money and influence that accompanies. Anyone who appreciates freedom and individual rights understands the danger of having these folks in charge, unchecked.

But the greater question is this: what is it about people that they have a need to be *led?* Why the historical attraction of kings? Why succumb to authoritarians? Sometimes even *ask* for them?

It seems to me that it must be rooted in our instinct for survival and in our emotion of fear. In times of anarchy; in times of war; in times of danger (both real and imagined), we often seek out a king or succumb to a tyrant. We seem to think it the lesser of two evils, the safer alternative. It never is.

Ben Franklin said, "They that can give up essential liberty to obtain a little temporary safety deserve neither liberty nor safety."

W. Somerset Maugham said, "If a nation values anything more than freedom, it will lose its freedom; and the irony of it is that if it is comfort or money that it values more, it will lose that, too."

And yet we panic; we clamor for kings. Folks with the need to lead create emergencies and crisis, some contrived and some

Lost American Principles: the Counter-revolution

real, like wars, disasters, and imminent "threats". They spread fear with the goal of obtaining more power for themselves.

H. L. Mencken said, "The whole aim of practical politics is to keep the populace alarmed - and hence clamorous to be led to safety - by menacing it with an endless series of hobgoblins, all of them imaginary."

Rahm Emmanuel, Barack Obama's Chief of Staff, said, "You never want a serious crisis to go to waste."

Daniel Webster said, "Good intentions will always be pleaded for any assumption of power. The Constitution was made to guard the people against the dangers of good intentions. There are men in all ages who mean to govern well, but they mean to govern. They promise to be good masters, but they mean to be *masters*."

And Rick Gaber observed, "No matter who you are or what you believe, you have to understand that someday the worst control-freaks among your bitterest enemies will control the federal government, and you better have restored effective, working constitutional limitations on that government before that time arrives."

Those with the need to lead are salivating for their opportunities, those times when the populace feels the need to be led. When that happens, the Rule of Law, and the constraints of our Constitution, are severely tested and stretched. Perhaps to the breaking point.

But freedom is not free. We cannot have both a king and a democratic process. The fantasy that we can have a king that will do whatever we ask him to do (democratically) is just that, a fleeting illusion. For tyranny will eventually be the result. If we truly desire freedom, peace, and prosperity, then, we must pay the price, we must work for it, we must meet our responsibilities voluntarily, and be ever vigilant against those who would be kings, those with the need to lead.

- - FPP - -

Chapter 9. Big, Bad Government

You hear a lot of talk about big government and too much government. But doesn't it make sense that we need as much government as it takes? And if we require lots of government, so be it? *We need as much government as is it takes to have a free, prosperous and peaceful country.* No more, because that is wasteful; no less, because we will not have attained freedom, prosperity and peace.

But now let us make a vital distinction. You see, "government" is simply the person or people that make the rules, and enforce them, for any given group. And there are two kinds of governments. There are folks who make the rules and enforce them - - governments - - in every church, organization, union, club, foundation, association, and corporation. There are hundreds of thousands of governments, large and small, everywhere.

These governments, call them little "g" governments, have several characteristics:

(1) membership in the group is voluntary, and therefore adherence to its rules is voluntary; that is, people are free to come and go;

(2) the rules are implemented without force; that is, violations of the rules might be punished by fines, demotions, suspensions, or even expulsion, but not by criminal prosecution;

(3) the government of the group does not have the power to force its members to fund the group; people who do not pay might be suspended, excluded or expelled, but not put in jail for failure to provide financial support.

In a word, the essence of these governments, and the groups they govern, is that they are *voluntary*.

There is a second type of government, the big "G" Governments (with Guns). They differ from little "g" governments in several important respects:

(1) adherence to the rules is not voluntary;

(2) the rules are enforced by police and soldiers with pistols, rifles, shotguns, clubs, and tazers, and with grenades, missiles, tanks, and bombs; violations of the rules are punished with criminal prosecutions and prisons, even death;

(3) the Government has the power to use that Force to extract its financial needs from the citizens, to tax them and/or confiscate their property and possessions.

In a word, the essence of big "G" Governments is *Force*.

So the actual "size", the total amount, of government does not really matter, as long as there is enough government to achieve freedom, peace and prosperity (and not more). But it matters a great deal how much of that governance is achieved voluntarily. And how much is accomplished by Force.

Big "G" Government's only tool is Force. Can we really expect to beat the Peace into people? To use laws to force Prosperity? Can we use guns to violate one person's individual Rights for some higher purpose and still call ourselves a Free people? Of course not, no, and absolutely not.

George Washington said it well, "Government is not reason. Government is not eloquence. It is force. Like fire, it is a dangerous servant and a fearful master!"

Free people, with their individual Rights protected, and then doing what they do naturally, is what produces prosperity. Thus, the best, the healthiest, the most productive governance is achieved voluntarily, through little "g" governments. This is where the "liberals" often go wrong; they fail to recognize the vast superiority of voluntary solutions, through voluntary governments. They often have a misplaced trust in the Force of Governments (with Guns), believing that somehow they can use that deadly force, not just to protect, but also to mold the world to some higher ideal.

John F. Kennedy, in accepting the nomination of the Liberal Party in 1960, said *"I do not favor state compulsion when voluntary individual effort can do the job and do it well."*

The "conservatives", however, make an equally grave mistake. You see, individual Rights are the key to freedom, prosperity and peace. And those Rights must be guarded as tenaciously as a mother bear guards her cubs. But every Right, by its very existence, defines corresponding Responsibilities; Rights and Responsibilities are two sides of the same coin. So when those Responsibilities are not being met voluntarily, through little "g" governments, then it is the proper place for

Government to step in and use its Force to meet those Responsibilities. In fact, the Government has an *obligation* to do so.

An example: Our most precious right is the Right to Life. But that Right simultaneously defines and creates Responsibilities for those who would enjoy it. Because if we have a Right to live, we also have a Right to keep living, to survive. Sure, we need protection from those who would take our lives, but we also need food, potable water, clothing, shelter, sewage systems, and basic health care in order to survive. So these things become the Responsibility, in a free society, of those that have to provide for those that do not. That is, if we are truly free and want to remain that way. And when the little "g" governments, the churches and organizations and foundations and corporations and the like, fail to meet these needs, voluntarily, then we get what we deserve, Government forcing us to do so. In other words, it costs us some of our Freedom when we do not meet our Responsibilities.

This creates a great deal of political friction. Democrats accuse Republicans of being cold and heartless when it comes to those citizens who are lacking in the basic needs for survival. And Republicans accuse Democrats of using the power of Force in excess, and confiscating too many resources from the citizens. But they are both correct.

The conservatives need to acknowledge the Responsibility of a free people to ensure not just that every citizen can experience life, but also that they can continue to live. And the liberals need to understand that meeting these needs voluntarily is far superior to the use of Force and guns and laws and confiscation.

But can't Government "partner" with the voluntary governments to meet those responsibilities? To answer that question, let's try a couple of examples. You have two dissenting livestock associations, the sheep growers and the cattlemen. They agree to put down their arms and hire a sheriff to keep the peace. But what happens if the sheriff goes into partnership with the cattlemen?

Or, at the time of this writing, it is March Madness in the college basketball world. The NCAA hires referees to keep the game in control, basically to protect each player's right to a

Lost American Principles: the Counter-revolution

level playing field, to enforce the rules. But what if the referee partners up with one of the teams? Or actually plays for one team during the game?

You see, the Government cannot partner, join, or otherwise participate in Free activities without bringing their Force, and their Guns, to that activity. Because then that voluntary activity is no longer a matter of free choice; rather, the freedom to choose is inhibited. Thus if a country is to be Free, and if the goals are Freedom, Prosperity, and Peace, then Governments must: (1) allow and encourage voluntary governments, and lower levels of Government, to meet our Responsibilities; (2) use their power of Force only as a last resort; (3) avoid the lethal temptation to partner with voluntary governments; and, (4) when the Government does find it necessary to involve itself, get out of that activity at the first opportunity, turning the reins back over to voluntary governments, or at least to lower levels of Government.

Those who benefit most from our freedoms, and from free markets, also then bear the greatest Responsibility and ought to be leading the charge. Voluntarily. That eliminates the need for Governments to intervene in the first place. And if the Government has already taken over a Responsibility, simply step in and start doing it better, *displacing* the need for them to be there. After all, we know that free and voluntary governments operate better, cheaper and more efficiently, and can do the job better, yes?

And those who prosper need to also use some discipline, contain their greed, when it appears that "partnering" with the Government will benefit them or give them an economic advantage. Short-termer's disease is pandemic, and deadly.

Thus little "g" voluntary governments need to see that every American citizen can survive; that is, has access to food, water, clothing, shelter, sewage systems, and basic health care. (The work done by the voluntary governments is charity rather than welfare. The Welfare provided by Government is a signal that those who are enjoying the fruits of freedom are not voluntarily meeting their corresponding obligations.   Welfare is Force; charity is voluntary.) Charity is the price of our Freedom, the Responsibility side of that coin. And most religions tell us we have that obligation as well.

We will address some of the other Right/Responsibility pairs a bit later. But it is important to remember: the "how big" in relation to government is not the real issue, what matters is how many of our Responsibilities are met voluntarily - - in an ideal world, all of them - - so that the only work left for the Federal Government (with its Guns) is protecting our Rights and national defense.

- - FPP - -

Chapter 10. The Bully

Suppose there is a neighborhood Bully. Things must be done his way. Plus, he is big enough and strong enough to impose his will by force whenever he thinks it necessary. *Does force make his decisions right?*

You are fifteen years old. One day, after school, you talk to a classmate that is considered an outsider, dresses weird and seems different; but you have a good conversation. The Bully sees you talking. And decides that you need to be locked in a closet in the abandoned warehouse every afternoon for two hours, from the time school is out until it's time to go home.

Now the Bully actually has very good intentions. He believes that this is in your best interests, to keep you from falling in with this "troublemaker", to keep you safe. And you are not powerful enough to fight the bully, nor to resist. But, *does that make him right?*

(Some might be a bit more cynical, thinking maybe the Bully has his own designs on your new friend.)

Ah, but now suppose the Bully is none other than a family member. In fact, he is your own Uncle Wilson. This does not change the fact that he is a Bully, or that he can use force to impose his will, but *does being a family member make him right?*

And, truth be known, Uncle Wilson is the most successful, the most respected, and the most loved member of your family. He always brings gifts when he visits. He never forgets birthdays, always calls and sends a card with some money enclosed. Uncle Wilson usually buys the best Christmas presents under the tree. And he always has hugs and smiles and kind words at family gatherings.

So, here is the real question: Does Uncle Wilson, as the bearer of goodwill and goodies, and with the best of intentions, have the right to force you, against your will (and without your parents' permission), to spend afternoons locked up in that closet? *Or is that, still, just the act of a Bully?*

The Bully

In 1961, Congress officially recognized "Uncle Sam" as America's National Symbol, a nickname that had been in use for some time. (The original "Uncle Wilson" was actually a man named Uncle Samuel Wilson, which, over time, was shortened to simply "Uncle Sam".)

And it seems to me that even our Uncle Sam, regardless of the best of intentions, no matter the ends, cannot and must not use force to violate our Rights. Even if he is big enough and strong enough to impose his will.

When your individual Rights are not fiercely guarded and defended, then the power of force can be used arbitrarily. This time, you are merely being locked in a closet. Next time, it may be something far more threatening. Or sinister.

Force does not make right. Only the rule of law, law that recognizes natural, unalienable, individual rights, can prevent the power of force from being turned against us. Only the Rule of Law, adhered to, can keep us free from the whims of a Bully. And there are plenty of Bullies out there to defend against, some with the very best of intentions, others not so much.

- - FPP - -

Chapter 11. Traffic Laws

Some people believe that we do not need Government. That we could live peacefully and prosperously without granting, or allowing, any Government the use of force. It seems a very problematic proposition.

First, consider that there are always people who will try to violate our individual rights and liberties. And without defense, the meanest brutes, or the bullies with the biggest clubs and most powerful weapons, will be able to commit these violations. Stealing, raping, killing, plundering, censorship, and exploitation are either uncontrolled; or, more likely, are tightly controlled and administered by authoritarians, through the use of deadly force. That is what happens in neighborhoods overtaken by gangs. That is what happens in countries ruled by kings, dictators and tyrants.

Second, every country has a Government, so how we would reach that point of no government? There are two options, it seems. The first is through a Government that is designed to put all the pieces in place and then disappear, to exert enough control to eliminate all obstacles and then just wither away, leaving a happy populace. Wait – isn't that what Communism was supposed to do? That didn't work out very well, did it? Most Communist countries have gone broke trying to get there; the remaining ones have not been able to shed their (totalitarian-style) Government and never will.

The other option, if we were to be without Government, is anarchy. This requires folks to rise up and overthrow the Government. But consider a mutiny at sea, where the sailors toss out an incompetent captain. Who is in charge then? Is everyone a co-captain? Hardly - because inevitably someone, through guile and through force, takes over control. Same with anarchy; in the resulting chaos, someone, backed with military force, takes the reins and does so in a dictatorial fashion. So we are right back to the brutes and bullies.

Think about driving your car into a large city with no traffic laws (no "automobile Government", if you will). Do you really believe that all the drivers would recognize everyone else's rights? Drive safely and courteously? That traffic would flow?

Traffic Laws

Of course not. We know that stop lights and traffic control signals help protect everyone. And without enforcement (en-*force*-ment), even these will not be obeyed by everyone.

An automobile becomes a deadly weapon when driven recklessly. The 30-06 hunting rifle produces nearly 3,000 foot-pounds of deadly force as the bullet leaves the barrel. A medium-sized car at just 35 miles per hour produces some 80,000 foot-pounds upon impact. The rifle bullet is more focused, of course, but the car can be just as deadly, and can more easily kill more than one person upon impact.

So yes, we need traffic laws. And we need sufficient Government to enforce them. In order guarantee our freedom to drive where we please and to protect against threats to our safety, perhaps our lives.

It seems to me the premise of no Government is an unreachable star, at least until humans are more perfect and peaceful beings. Certainly the ideals expressed in John Lennon's song *Imagine* are something we should work towards. Maybe someday humans will achieve it. But in the meantime, Government is essential. And we need to think about the best way to structure and control our Governments. And how we might establish a Government that has sufficient power to protect our Rights and Liberties, but at the same time constrains the people who Govern from going too far, denying them the temptation to use that power of deadly force against their own citizens, to violate individual Rights and Liberties rather than defend them.

- - FPP - -

Chapter 12. Flawed Folks

What do we *do* with them, the people who steal, cheat and lie? And the flawed folks who hurt others?

Well, first we need to accept a simple truth: all of us are flawed. In the sixth century, Pope Gregory I revised the list of deadly sins to include these seven: lust, gluttony, greed, sloth, wrath, envy, and pride. We know that throughout history humans have raped and fornicated; been greedy gluttons; robbed, lied, and manipulated; been apathetic, joyless, and lazy; have murdered and extracted revenge; been selfish, jealous, hateful, and envious; and have been vain and prideful.

Are we hopeless beasts? Depends on your view of things. Because we humans have also practiced chastity, temperance, charity, diligence, patience, kindness and humility. We have loved and helped one another. We have sometimes respected the fact that other individuals have the same Rights as we do. We are a mixed bag, we humans.

Is there any hope? Well, Christians believe that God can forgive our sins. And does. But, does the saved sinner then stop sinning? Are all of the sinner's undesirable impulses, thoughts and desires suddenly gone? Of course not. Most of the saints were not revered for their sudden lack of appetite, but for their ability to resist, to refuse to act upon their urges. The point is that we humans all have undesirable urges, built-in to our very makeup, for whatever reasons. And occasionally we succumb. So what do we do with us flawed folks?

Virtually every church in America accepts sinners; in fact, most encourage sinners to join. And when church members falter, commit sins, digress, or commit crimes, does the church punish them? Jail them? Execute them? No. (At least, not any more.) Sometimes, of course, the church will boot them out, but most often the church says to the sinner, "ask for forgiveness and we will forgive you".

It is so puzzling then, that many Christians are the first to ask their Government to punish, jail, and execute the sinners. And especially ironic when the "sin" has hurt no one but the sinner himself, or herself. It would seem that those "sins" are between that person and God.

Flawed Folks

Saint Thomas Aquinas said, "Because of the diverse conditions of humans, it happens that some acts are virtuous to some people, as appropriate and suitable to them, while the same acts are immoral to other people . . . "

Geoffrey Fisher, Archbishop of Canterbury, said "In a civilized society, all crimes are likely to be sins, but most sins are not and ought not to be treated as crimes. Man's ultimate responsibility is to God alone."

Gandhi observed "Truth resides in every human heart, and one has to search for it there . . . But no one has a right to coerce others to act according to his own view of the truth."

And Justice Oliver Wendell Holmes said "The aim of the law is <u>not</u> to punish sins."

Free people cannot hand over their individual Rights to Government. Thus, when it comes to adults committing acts which hurt no one but themselves, even if individuals had the right to punish these acts, they cannot give that right to their Government. The question becomes: do individuals have the *responsibility* to punish acts by their fellow citizens, when those acts hurt no one else? The answer (no!) is pretty apparent when you see that the voluntary governments in churches do not do so. And even if they did, would you want the Federal Government involved?

Abraham Lincoln said, "A prohibition law strikes a blow at the very principles upon which our government was founded. Prohibition goes beyond the bounds of reason in that it attempts to control a man's appetites by legislation, and makes a crime out of things that are not crimes."

Thomas Jefferson said, "The legitimate powers of government extend to such acts as are only injurious to others."

Why, *why*, WHY can't the "religious right" understand these principles? They seem to know that Government cannot *force* people to be prosperous, that freedom is the only thing that works in the marketplace. And yet they cling to this idea that Government can somehow force people to become moral (both at home and abroad). So they insist on laws that punish even those who are hurting no one but themselves. And in the process, they actually destroy our liberties.

And they war against other "evil" nations, filled with "less-than-human" citizens. But doing so destroys any real chance of world peace.

Laws that *protect* individual Rights and Liberties, of course, do not fall into this category. When someone hurts another, or violates their freedom, then it is time for Government to intervene on behalf of the victim; that is the reason we have Government. Likewise when crimes are committed against children, or others who do not have the capacity for free choice. But when adults voluntarily act in a manner which hurts no one but themselves, then that is between those persons, their conscience, and their God.

The bottom line is this: humans are flawed. And any system of Government whose success is dependent upon a populace of unflawed people, the elected or the electors, is doomed to fail. The only Government that will succeed over the long-term is one that recognizes (a) that the citizens have weaknesses as well as strengths; and (b) that those who Govern also have weaknesses and strengths. The use of force must be limited to protecting individual Rights; and, dealing with those who violate a person's Rights.

Thus the tricky problem that our founders struggled with: how to balance democracy against tyranny. How to turn the use of deadly force over to a higher Government without having that Government then use that same force against the people themselves. Their solution was the rule of law, a constitutional Republic. And they wrote a contract between the people, the States, and the Federal Government which limited the powers of that Federal Government and included a system of divided responsibilities, and of checks and balances.

- - FPP - -

Chapter 13. Democracy

All people are flawed, to one extent or another. Thus having a simple majority rule by us flawed folks, with our decisions carried out though deadly force, can be problematic. That is what happens in a pure Democracy, where a majority vote of the people directly determines the laws of the land. The problem: 66 people can vote to violate the rights of the other 34.

Or, 99 people can vote to sacrifice another person for the "greater good", for some "higher purpose".

Thomas Jefferson said, "A Democracy is nothing more than mob rule, where fifty-one percent of the people may take away the rights of the other forty-nine."

James Bovard made this observation, "Democracy must be something more than two wolves and a sheep voting on what to have for dinner."

And John Adams said, "Remember, democracy never lasts long. It soon wastes, exhausts and murders itself. There never was a democracy yet that did not commit suicide."

But wait a minute, isn't democracy a warm-fuzzy concept? Doesn't democracy involve freedom, participation, and voting? Isn't it in democracies that people are equal, that the citizens appreciate and tolerate differences?

Time to differentiate. Yes, little "d" democracy is the essence of freedom. A Government of, by, and for the people is a Fundamental Principle; that *is* democracy. Elections and voting are the means for making a representative Government work.

But no, forming a big "D" Democracy, where the majority rule is the *only* law, the Law of the Land, is not conducive to freedom, or to individual rights. That's what Jefferson and Bovard were warning us against.

Here is an example: when the majority of folks realize that they can vote to get favors from the public trough, they usually do. One group uses the Government to forcefully transfer wealth from others to themselves. In fact, I have read that today, the *majority* of Americans collect more in direct benefits from Government than they pay in.

And when a majority of the people become frightened and fear for their safety, they often clamor to violate the rights of the minority, like when we jailed (Japanese) American citizens during World War Two. Or like passing a Patriot Act after 9/11.

Our founders struggled with this contradiction. And they decided that while they wanted a democracy, as opposed to another King, they needed somehow to protect the Rights of the minorities. So they wrote a contract between themselves and the new Government, the Constitution, that attempted not only to acknowledge the unalienable Rights of individual citizens, but also to provide a system of checks and balances so that those Rights could not be violated.

Thus America was founded as a Republic. A nation of laws. Managed and operated little "d" democratically, of course: of the people, by the people, and for the people. But under a law of the land that defended the individual Rights of each and every citizen. *Even when the majority voted to violate them.* (We are not necessarily talking about majority races here; we are talking about a majority of the people.)

But all governments, no matter how arrived at, are composed of people. And people being what they are, they too often yield to the temptation to wield the force of Government against the minority, usually to some "higher purpose". The power to control others is self-reinforcing; that is, it often leads the powerful to conclude that they *must* control others. For their own good. And then violating the Rights of a certain group of people is justified as a small price for them to pay when it will "benefit the greater society". Thus, the powerful often rationalize ("rational lies") illegal or immoral means to accomplish their lofty ends. It is true that power can corrupt.

Wendell Phillips said, "Governments exist to protect the rights of minorities. The loved and the rich need no protection; they have many friends and few enemies."

Little "d" democracy is indeed a trademark of freedom. And is at its best in voluntary governments like churches and organizations. But when we are considering handing the power of deadly force over to a Democracy as the sole structure of a Government, we must proceed with extreme caution. Somehow the Rights of the minority must be protected and guarded, or they will be violated. In fact, if a people are to be free, the first responsibility of their Government is the defense of their individual Rights. To understand this concept, we only need to look at countries who have democratically voted in tyrants, who have freely chosen leaders that abuse, and even kill, the very people who elected them.

Where does America stand today? Well, the Republic is pretty battered. The laws spelled out in our Constitution are routinely broken. Individual Rights have become more like privileges, for our Government to provide or take away as they deem fit, in our "best interests". In the beginning, many politicians served humbly, viewing their service in office as a civic duty, putting in their time and then letting the next person take over. Most understood that their obligation was to the law of the land and to the Constitution, not to the latest whim or fad. Nor to the demands of an emotional mob.

But today, we have *professional* Politicians. Today, they must do *whatever it takes* to keep their jobs, to get re-elected. They poll constantly, they test the ever-shifting winds of public opinion, and they provide the majority with whatever they demand, even if it means violating their oath of office, or the Constitution. And if they satisfy our demands for goodies, then we re-elect them. Thus we have, in many ways, become more of a true Democracy than a Republic. And the Rights of minorities are routinely breeched.

So Democracies can easily self-destruct. When the majority wields sufficient force that it can violate whatever individual Rights is chooses, then that Government has become, in effect, a tyranny. And usually, at some point in the downward slide, the mob pleads for an authoritarian, or allows a tyrant, to take over. Our founders feared Democracy, as the structure of a Government, for that reason.

C.S. Lewis said, "Of all tyrannies, a tyranny sincerely exercised for the good of its victims may be the most oppressive. It would be better to live under robber barons than under omnipotent moral busybodies. The robber baron's cruelty may sometimes sleep, his cupidity may at some point be satiated; but those who torment us for our own good will torment us without end, for they do so with the approval of their own conscience."

Lost American Principles: the Counter-revolution

But while democracy has within it the seeds of its own destruction, it also has the seeds for its redemption. There are both weeds and flowers in this garden, and while the weeds have just about taken over, there still might be an opportunity for the flowers of freedom to break through.

Here is why. While the majority of Americans might receive more benefits from their Government than they pay in; and while that leads to them voting for even more goodies from the public trough, the fact is that the public is also apathetic. Less than half of Americans usually vote.

So it is not really the majority of people that controls, it is the *majority of voters*. The political majority. Think about it: if 40% of the folks vote in an election, then it only takes 21% of the population to win that election. As Jesse Jackson said, "In politics, an organized minority is a political majority."

So it is not as hopeless as it sometimes feels or seems. We only need to rally up maybe a fourth of us, working together, voting, exercising our *democratic* responsibilities, to effect some real change. In the end, democracy can work for us. And then perhaps we can install some additional safeguards so that it does not work against us.

Democracy, like fire, can be either beneficial and essential; or, it can be dangerous and destructive. It all depends on how it is used, and whether sufficient safeguards are maintained so that it does not get out of control. While essential to our well-being, if unchecked it can quickly become a deadly force, burn down its own house, destroy its own freedom.

- - FPP - -

Chapter 14. Four Dreams

<u>The first dream</u>: I dreamed that I was King. My every whim was indulged. I enjoyed bountiful feasts and music, dancers and clowns and musicians, exotic sights and scents and sounds. I had my choice of the most beautiful women in the Kingdom. Emissaries from far and wide presented me with lavish gifts; they kneeled and kissed my feet when they approached me. And the people bowed when I passed.

I was a fair and just King; I could not be otherwise, because my power came from God. I named princes and administrators to rule the land and to enforce my laws. I understood the need for separation of the various classes of people; I defined the classes, and the rights and opportunities of each. I beheaded the enemies of the Empire and purged the people that were a scourge in my Kingdom. I enslaved the unworthy, but allowed them the honor of building great castles and pyramids and monuments in my name.

I eliminated the blasphemous, and the false religions that they preached; I required that everyone follow the true religion. I ensured that all speeches and books were supportive of me; I severely punished those who would criticize me. I decided what property my subjects were entitled to, seizing that which would better serve the needs of my Kingdom.

And I knew that my God-given sovereignty over man required me to conquer the world and to extend my Empire to the far corners of the earth. I sent my armies into every nation; if the people acknowledged my sovereignty, I welcomed them under my rule. If they refused, I had them tortured, crucified, and killed, or I enslaved them. All was good; it was as God willed it. I knew that I had jealous enemies and that some craved my power, but my advisors and informants allowed me to keep them at bay.

But then I noticed movements in the shadows. Dark figures were creeping toward me, surrounding my throne. I could see the outline of the knives in their hands. And as I saw one of those knives thrusting toward my heart, I awoke with a start.

Lost American Principles: the Counter-revolution

<u>The second dream</u>: I dreamed that I was the Leader. We had taken over the Government, with the dream of creating a perfect social society. Where everyone was happy and industrious and prosperous.

We hated capitalism and all that it stood for. We knew that individual "human rights" were an illusion, a trap invented by the greedy capitalists as a means to enslave the populace. We had a higher purpose, a plan to implement a system that would result in the greater good for all society. We called ourselves communists, although some used the term socialist.

I was a fair and just leader; I could not be otherwise, because everything I did was for the greater good. I named administrators and generals to rule the land and to enforce my laws. I decided where people would work and where they would live; and, who was entitled to special privileges and opportunities. I jailed the enemies of the state and eliminated the people that were a scourge in our country.

I eradicated the blasphemous, and the false religions that they preached. I took over the press and the media; I severely punished those who would criticize me. I controlled what was taught in school. I decided what property my subjects were entitled to, seizing that which would better serve the needs of the state. I controlled all trade and production and money and prices.

And I knew that our vision required us to conquer the world and to extend our empire to the far corners of the earth. I sent my armies into surrounding nations; we conquered them and snuffed out their evil capitalistic habits.

We knew that once the people were happy and productive, after we had forced them to experience the greater good - - as soon as they were all good people - - that our Government would fade away.

But in the shadows I saw long lines, poverty, and want. A dismal gray pallor was enveloping the country. And then I saw the walls crumbling above me and I awoke with a start.

<u>The third dream</u>: I dreamed that we had overthrown the Government. Because the people who governed had violated justice, legislating and taxing illegally. "For the greater good,"

Four Dreams

they had always claimed, of course, but in effect no different than the tyrants and socialists that had gone before.

So we had staged a successful coup and ousted everyone in the Government. We were in the process of dismantling every last vestige of the sprawling bureaucracies and the networks of law enforcement. We would now live free.

We were establishing a perfect anarchy, where the only law was the law of justice, and justice endowed us with our rights. Our only requirement was to live honestly. As Lysander Spooner * taught us, "no man can delegate . . . [any] legislative power whatever - - over himself or anybody else, to any man, or body of men." Thus the Constitution and taxes were both invalid and illegal in the first place.

We knew that when the people were honest and practiced justice - - as soon as they were all good people - - that Government would never again be required.

But in the shadows I noticed a commotion. Dishonest people began to ignore the law of justice, stealing, looting, and killing. Blood and chaos spilled into the streets. And armies were approaching our shores. People began crying out for a king, a savior. I ducked behind a wall at the sound of gunfire and looked up to see a plane releasing a bomb overhead, and I awoke with a start.

[*note: For more information about Lysander Spooner, please refer to the Chapter Notes, on page 159]

The fourth dream: I dreamed that I lived in a free land, where every person was deemed equal and where each had individual rights, Rights that *no one* could take away. We had secured these Rights through the Rule of Law, with a Constitution, and we had thus experienced greater prosperity than any other country in history.

We had long ago discarded the idea of the divine rights of kings. We disdained the idea of any Government - - authoritarian, tyrant, ruler, dictator, whatever the title and no matter how it came to power - - using deadly force against its own citizens, in order to take away their natural, individual Rights. *We had chosen the Rule of Law, rather than the laws of rulers.*

Lost American Principles: the Counter-revolution

We had said "no" to the socialists and communists who preached that individuals had neither value nor rights, that they were merely contributors to a greater good, and were thus dispensable. They taught that our society must operate like an anthill or a colony of bees. We knew that such denials of individual rights and freedoms would only restrain the positive forces of human nature and would inevitably lead to nothing more than shared misery and shared poverty. With a powerful, privileged elite at the controls.

We had said "no" to the anarchists who believed in the "science of justice", a science that said that we had no individual rights except those derived from justice. That's backwards, we realized; justice evolves from natural, individual rights. [Note: In the earliest years of the science of astronomy, much the same error was made. The world, they discovered, was not flat. But the scientists mistakenly taught that the sun and moon revolved around the earth, rather than the other way around, which led to terribly erroneous conclusions.] So while the anarchists believe that we cannot legally have either Government or taxes, because both violate their science of justice, at the same time they admit that until all folks are honest, we will be in a constant state of war.

We had declared to the world our Idea of America: that each and every person had equal, unalienable, natural Rights to life, liberty, and the pursuit of happiness. We initiated the national Government through a contract, the Constitution, which established the Rule of Law and limited Government powers, a Government with democracy as its engine, but a Federal Republic as its structure. In so doing, human energy was released in a way unprecedented in history.

But in the shadows I saw that a quiet *revolution* had taken place, nearly unnoticed. In the course of less than a hundred years, the authoritarians and the socialists among us had mutinied, step-by-step, against the Rule of Law, against our own Constitution. The American experiment was falling apart. While a revolutionary war had freed us from the King, it seemed that we could not rinse that sweet taste of blood from our lips; we were a warrior nation. And we had become an empire, following in the steps of the kings and tyrants and communists throughout history, becoming, to other countries, the same sort of power that we had revolted against. Like all empires, we had reached the point of unsustainable debt, and our economy was rotting from within. The anarchists were preparing for battle. I tried to awaken, but I realized that this was no dream . . .

Waking up: Four dreams of Government - how do they resonate with our goals of Freedom, Peace and Prosperity?

The anarchists believe that we can achieve Freedom and Prosperity without Government. But until all people (or nearly all) are honest, and follow the laws of justice, then we will be at war. As Lysander Spooner put it, "[when men commit crimes against the property or persons of others, then] men are at war. And they must necessarily remain at war until justice is reestablished." So the anarchists would sacrifice Peace in order to obtain Freedom and Prosperity.

The socialists believe that we can achieve Peace and Prosperity, but only at the expense of Freedom. And until all people are (*forced* to be) happy and industrious, there will be no freedom from a totalitarian-type Government. In other words, the socialists would sacrifice Freedom in order to obtain Peace and Prosperity.

Neither anarchists nor socialists seem to acknowledge that all people are flawed, to some degree, even those who Govern. (And humans probably will be flawed for some time to come, for at least a few more centuries, don't you think?) So, in the case of the anarchists, there will never be Peace, without Government. Likewise, the socialists would never be able to shake off the chains of Government; they would never achieve any degree of Freedom. In other words, both of these theories require some nirvana occupied by near-perfect people in order to achieve all three: freedom, peace, and prosperity.

The authoritarians, of course, would decide and define themselves what constitutes freedom, peace, and prosperity. And who gets it. Privileges, yes; rights, no. The favored benefit, while most of the people, most of the time, have little. Since they are merely flawed mortals like the rest of us, their decisions are subject to their own jealousies, greed, whims, insecurities, and weaknesses, and can change like the winds. In other words, while people often yearn for a King, he would have to be a permanently-perfect person if the populace would achieve freedom, peace, and prosperity.

The only viable alternative is to form a Government whose only job is to defend individual Rights. To guarantee individual Liberties. And to ensure that people follow the fundamental principle of the Golden Rule, free to do as they please as long as they do not infringe on someone else's right to do the same. That Freedom, thus protected, is what *produces* Prosperity. And establishes the framework for Peace, inside a country.

To establish Peace externally, the same principles apply. Allowing our neighbors, every country, their own Sovereignty, to do as they please as long as they do not infringe on another country's right to do the same. Never doing to another country what you would not tolerate them doing to you. Live and let live.

The things we do not want done to us, as individuals, are the same things that other countries resent: meddling; deciding and defining for others how they should act; favoritism; deadly force used by authoritarians (subject to jealousies, greed, whims, insecurities and weaknesses, and changing every 4 or 8 years, like the winds) . . . these lead inevitably to war. And War is *always* destructive, in countless ways, of our own Freedom, Peace, and Prosperity.

Peace can only happen when the Government of a country respects the rights of other countries. We had such a Government; or, perhaps I should say that we attempted it. George Washington eloquently explained to us these principles of external Peace. But we ignored his advice. We have allowed ourselves to get into the empire-building business, and simultaneously, in the last 90 years or so, the socialists and authoritarians have staged a quiet revolution against our own Rule of Law and our Constitution.

So Peace is gone, and seems out of reach; we seem destined to un-winnable and eternal war. Our Prosperity has eroded; the last 30 years, in fact, have been a false prosperity, an illusion

Four Dreams

created by bubbles, and the bubbles are bursting. And our Freedom has been usurped. If we do not change course, we will soon reach the point of tyranny; it is inevitable. The anarchists are, of course, calling for a revolution. But that would only lead to more war, and in the end the folks with the biggest guns would assume power . . . result: tyranny.

The anarchists are wrong. We don't need a revolution, because the revolution has already begun; it is unfolding right before our eyes. The question is whether there are enough people willing to *counter* the revolution, to use democracy to put it down. Whether the American people are ready to take another run at the Idea of America and the Rule of Law. Whether "real change" is an ideal that we are willing to work for, or is just a Political slogan that encourages us down the same destructive path.

Real change is indeed needed. Now. So that we might have a real chance at Freedom, Peace, and Prosperity.

>*Instead* of worldwide economic upheaval.
>*Instead* of war.
>*Instead* of tyranny.

My dreams. But your decision.

- - FPP - -

Chapter 15. A Living, Breathing Document

Our Constitution is a living, breathing document. It can transform itself and adapt to the ever-changing world around us. It evolves constantly to meet unexpected challenges and to react to issues which could never have been anticipated. The framers intentionally designed it not to be "written in stone", like the Ten Commandments, but rather to be interpreted as conditions demand.

Wow. Awesome. What an incredible document! There is just one little, teeny, tiny problem with this premise: it is BS. Pure propaganda. Politi-speak at its worst. Rationalizing to the extreme ("rational lies"). And a thinly-veiled cover for violating our Constitution. Think about it, please - - they are basically saying that our Constitution allows them to do anything they wish, whatever *they* think is "best".

First of all, the Constitution is not just a "document"; it is a Contract. It was the Contract under which we the people granted power to the Government in the first place. It defines the meeting of the minds required for that Contract, and the conditions under which we would allow the Government to use its force.

Secondly, contracts are not "living"; the agreement cannot simply be changed by one side. What they are telling us is that the Government, one party to the Contract, can change the terms unilaterally, without the consent of the other parties (the States and the people).

Just imagine if all contracts were treated that way:

You sign a lease. One day your landlord shows up at your doorstep and informs you that he is increasing your rent. Substantially. Wait, you say, "We have a contract, a lease, that specifies the rent; it is fixed for the term of the lease." He replies, "Fixed rents are an outdated concept. We need to be able to raise the rents when we have unforeseen expenses."

Or you take out a loan to buy a car. One day the bank calls you and says that your payment is increasing. A bunch. Wait, you say, "We have a contract that specifies a fixed payment every month." And the banker replies, "Oh, the word "payment" in that document was designed and intended to be subject to interpretation, based on evolving conditions. Sure, when the loan was originally made, the payment amount was something we could both agree to, but now the world has changed and that payment is no longer appropriate."

Or you hire a contractor to remodel your kitchen. One day he shows up and says, "I have done A and B, but I cannot do C unless you pay me more money." Wait a minute, you say, "We signed a contract that says you would do A, B, and C for a specified amount of money. And I have already paid you. Either finish the job, or give me some of my money back." Well, the contractor says, "I have already spent the money, so I can't give you a refund. And that document was really just a set of guidelines. I was sincere when I gave you that price, but conditions are different now. Look - I need more money. So you have to pay it if you want the work done."

Don't you see how our whole economy, our whole world, would fall apart if contracts are not binding? If one party to the contract can "change the deal" without the consent of the other? If there is no enforcement of contracts?

So look – either the perpetrators of this nonsense about a living, breathing document do not believe that the Constitution is a Contract, the law of the land. Or they are somehow convinced that their view of the "greater good" is more important than following the law. In either case, we are in deep trouble, because if our Constitution is just to be interpreted "as needed", then, as the late George Carlin said, we really *have no rights*. All we have are permissions, permissions that can be granted or withdrawn as those with the Power deem "best" for us. Or for them.

[*footnote: The ability to freely contract, to voluntarily enter into binding, enforceable agreements, is simply an extension of individual Rights. Private Property Rights, for example, include the rights to hold and use property; to sell and trade that property; and to profit from it. And contracts allow that to happen in an orderly fashion, while protecting the rights of both parties.]

Lost American Principles: the Counter-revolution

While our Leaders take oaths of office, swearing on a Bible to uphold the Constitution, they routinely "interpret", and misinterpret, as they see fit. If you believe that the Constitution is binding, is a Contract, is the Rule of Law - - and not just a set of suggestions - - then you must realize that it is violated every day. Not just in insignificant ways, but in profound, freedom-robbing ways. Woods and Gutzman, in their book *Who Killed the Constitution?* say it bluntly, "The Constitution is Dead". *

Here's the problem. Our founders did not, could not, anticipate all of America's future challenges. (For example, they did not foresee a monopoly two-party system dominated by professional politicians.) But they knew that they did not have crystal balls and so they provided the means to change the law of the land as needed: by *amending* the Constitution. That's what happens with any contract that needs changing, it can be done when, and if, all of the parties agree to change it.

The framers divided the Government's powers into three distinct branches, so that each would provide a check on the other, each restricted to certain responsibilities. They carefully designed a system of checks and balances, in order to protect the other parties to the Constitution, the States and the people.

Still, many of the founders feared that these checks and balances would not be sufficient, that Government would use its force beyond the limits of the Constitution.

When asked what kind of Government they had formed, Benjamin Franklin said, "A Republic, ma'm, *if you can keep it*."

But Government has exceeded the limits placed upon it by the Constitution. Every branch. Presidents (the Executive Branch) have declared wars, spent taxpayer money, and effected laws, all violations of the Constitution.

Congress (the Legislative Branch) has passed un-Constitutional legislation, and ignored many of its responsibilities.

[*footnote: Thomas E. Woods. Jr. and Kevin R. C. Gutzman, New York Times Bestselling Authors, Crown Forum / Random House, Inc, 2008. A great read, by the way. Recommended.]

And the Supreme Court (the third branch) has unilaterally re-interpreted the Constitution and gotten into the lawmaking business itself.

In spite of the checks and balances, all three branches have ignored the law and exercised powers that they were never granted. Not always, of course - - in many cases, the checks kept the Government within its proper authority. But when one violation is allowed to stand, over time it becomes a precedent. An excuse for the next violation. And that for the next.

I don't think this was a "conspiracy" of the three branches, for that would require cooperation and common ideals that the professional politicians are simply not capable of. Rather, it is a loose "cartel", each branch conveniently ignoring the transgressions of the others at times. So that the other branches will ignore theirs. And each branch has neither the resolve, nor the courage, to make a stand; after all, it would require admitting their own crimes as well.

So - when all three branches of our Federal Government refuse to follow the Constitution, how can it be enforced? The answer is simple: it can't. Not lawfully. So in reality, in truth, if our Government does what it pleases, pretending to follow the Constitution while flagrantly ignoring it, then Woods and Gutzman are correct, the Constitution is dead.

But, as with a child pulled out of a swimming pool, who has stopped breathing and turned blue, could we not resuscitate? Should we not try? Perhaps, with a huge grassroots, democratic effort, we could breathe life back into the Constitution, reaffirm it, close up the loopholes, and add a Second Bill of Rights.

More specific violations, and some ideas for the necessary Constitutional amendments, are detailed in later chapters. But ponder this question once more: if all three branches of Government refuse to follow the terms of the Constitution, how can it be enforced? If we live under the Rule of Law, what do we do when that Rule of Law is violated, by the very people that are supposed to enforce it?

Here is a thought: perhaps by adding a fourth branch, the "missing branch", the States Branch. It was, after all, the States

Lost American Principles: the Counter-revolution

that originally agreed to form our national Government in the first place, to hand powers and responsibilities over to it; but the States have lost practically all control and now the Federal Government refuses to police itself.

So what if we did this: create one more branch of Federal Government, composed of two delegates from each State, one would be the Governor (or the Governor's appointee) and the other elected by the State Legislature. This body of one hundred would meet annually, or more often if necessary. It would not have any lawmaking authority; it would not have any budget authority. The *only* power the States Branch would have is veto power; that is, (with a super-majority vote?) it could veto any Federal legislation that it deemed un-Constitutional; and, it could halt any Federal acts that it deemed un-Constitutional. Maybe that would provide the missing check and balance that would preserve our Amended Constitution.

The last thing we want is a living, breathing Constitution. We want and need a solid, clear, enforceable Contract between the States, the people, and our Federal Government. The Rule of Law. The law of the land that protects the Rights of each and every citizen, regardless of race, color, creed, sexual preference, wealth, nationality, religious beliefs, fame, size, eating habits, physical attributes, poverty, lack of education, or any other means of classification. We want a Government that follows the Constitution and thus keeps us free. So that we can work toward true peace and real prosperity.

- - FPP - -

Chapter 16. The Perfect Constitution

Eleven years passed between the Declaration of Independence and the Constitution. The Declaration, in 1776, boldly stated that, "all men are created equal" and have "certain unalienable Rights." It was our formal explanation for why we had revolted against the King. Written (mostly) by Thomas Jefferson, the Declaration not only announced to the world that we were no longer colonies of the British Empire, but also asserted that natural law entitles people to Rights, including the Right to self-govern. Jefferson was eloquent in expressing the ideas of Freedom and democracy.

The Constitution was adopted in 1787, after much debate and discussion. It established a Federal Republic with limited and separated powers for the national Government. Curiously, in the Constitution, Jefferson's words - - the very reason for the existence of the new country - - were diluted, watered down: the Preamble to the Constitution merely says, "promote the general welfare and secure the blessings of liberty". *But what happened to our unalienable Rights?* Where is the statement that people are *equal?* Why leave out the concepts of self-governance? Why aren't the Principles that gave birth to our country enumerated in our Constitution?

Clearly, some two hundred years later, we can see that "promote the general welfare" has far different implications than "certain unalienable Rights". Here are some possible explanations as to why the revolutionary ideals in the Declaration of Independence (the *Idea* of America) were left out of the Constitution itself:

1. People understood the concepts and they were pretty much universally accepted. They may have thought, "We have a *Right* to life, liberty and the pursuit of happiness? Well, duh, that's why we just fought a war against the British Empire. Everybody knows that. We don't need to spell it out again when we describe the structure of our new Government."

2. Slavery pretty much contradicted the "all men are created equal" idea. Look – slavery had been with us for all of recorded history. I think I even recall that in the Bible, God's chosen people conquered other tribes and took them into slavery - - the ones they did not kill - - with God's blessing. But by the

1700's, the whole idea of slaves was becoming distasteful; the immorality of it was growing apparent. People were coming to their senses: slavery was ugly, evil, cruel, hideous . . . and just plain wrong.

But how to end slavery was another story. Like an obese person who has made a commitment to lose weight, there is a lot of struggle and pain ahead. Writing down the goal, vowing to get there, is different than having someone follow you around with a club to smack you when you eat improperly.

So maybe the specific language of the Declaration was watered down in order to keep the Southern States on board. In retrospect, it might have been better to include those Fundamental Principles in the Constitution and then not allow States to join the Union unless, and until, they had cleaned up their act. Ah, but we are so often willing to sacrifice our Liberty for a little "safety". Perhaps the promise of a national defense, and a larger nation, seemed to outweigh the "unalienable Rights" of individuals.

3. We might not have had a Constitution without the compromise. People often view our Constitution with reverence, as if the document were an inspired revelation, as if God visited Philadelphia and handed it down on clay tablets, as if the framers were in unanimous, illuminated agreement as they wrote.

It is hardly any of that. The Constitution is a compromise, the result of a battle of ideas and ideals. The founders were mere mortals, flawed like the rest of us. They did the best they could with what they knew at the time. And the American experiment that resulted has been a spectacular story. But is it perfect? Of course not.

There were basically three competing philosophies at the time. (Actually there were five, but we will discount the two that called for no Constitution at all: those who wanted the States to remain completely independent, with no national Government; and, those who wanted a new King for America.)

There were the Federalists, who wanted a very strong central Government (ala Alexander Hamilton). They were opposed by the anti-federalists, who wanted a very limited federal Government (ala Thomas Jefferson). And there was a compromise position, best represented by James Madison, the "father of the Constitution".

Hamilton's story is particularly interesting, especially because he is, today, becoming more popular. He was an authoritarian who believed that most of the power should reside in the central government.* He promoted, for example, a national bank. His idea for America was a quasi-monarchy, a central government with almost king-like powers, but with checks and balances through the Constitution. He mistrusted the judgment of individuals.

Jefferson, on the other hand, believed in individual Rights and in limited federal powers. Many of the anti-federalists thought that the federal Government should have less power than the States, perhaps even equal powers, but never more. And many argued that our specific individual Rights needed to be enumerated in the Constitution itself.

Madison was the chief architect of the compromise Constitution, the one that was finally agreed to. But it required ratification by the States in order to become law. And it did not have enough support; there were too many Jeffersonian anti-federalists that mistrusted the amount of power granted to the central Government. It looked like it would not be ratified.

That put Hamilton in an awkward position. Although he favored even more power for the central Government than what the compromise granted, he realized that if it was not ratified, if the anti-federalists defeated it, that he would then wind up with even less central power. So he joined Madison (and Jay) in a massive PR campaign in support of the Constitution, what we call the Federalist Papers, of which he is the chief author.
This was disingenuous on Hamilton's part, defending a Constitution that he felt afforded more central power than the people generally wanted, while re-assuring the populace, the anti-federalists, that their Rights were adequately protected.

Jefferson understood the hypocrisy, which led to a bitter rivalry between the two men.

[*footnote: see Chapter Notes for more on Hamilton's beliefs, p.159]

Lost American Principles: the Counter-revolution

The rest is history, as they say. The Federalist-Paper campaign convinced enough folks to support ratification (that is, on the express condition that the Bill of Rights would be added). Still, one must question Hamilton's arguments and motives. Were "all men are created equal" and our "unalienable Rights" left out intentionally? Did he know that the Constitution would prove inadequate to protect against virtually unlimited Federal powers? (Which is what he wanted.) Do you suppose that he foresaw the place we find ourselves in today?

The Constitution is not perfect. Probably never will be. But it is, supposedly, the law of the land, the ultimate authority for the Rule of Law. And it does have provisions for Amendment. Don't you think it is time to re-affirm the Constitution; to add a Second Bill of Rights; to pass Amendments that specify our fundamental ideals and explicitly state that all people are equal; and to include an Amendment that codifies our individual Rights to Life, Liberty and the Pursuit of Happiness?

By the way, I recently found out that my idea for a Second Bill of Rights is not entirely original, even though I have been promoting it for some years now. When I searched the web, I found that President Franklin D. Roosevelt had actually proposed a Second Bill of Rights. (I have never said that all of his ideas were bad.)

In any case, for whatever reasons, the principles that were the Idea of America, expressed in our Declaration of Independence, were left out of our Constitution. Let's put them in now. Before it's too late.

- - FPP - -

Chapter 17. Freedom, but not Free

Look - it's easy to exercise our Rights and our Liberties. They come naturally to us. As naturally as eating, for example. But as we know, when we are free to eat whatever and whenever we want to, we also have to practice some self-discipline. Otherwise we can become fat, even obese, lethargic and disinterested . . . downright unhealthy.

With Rights, we must also discipline ourselves by meeting the Responsibilities that come attached to each Right. When we do not, one of two things happens, either (a) we have a less-peaceful, less-prosperous society; or, (b) Government steps in to meet the Responsibilities for us - - that's their job - - and we have a less-free society. The country can easily become bloated with bureaucracy, even obese, and the people become lethargic and disinterested . . . very unhealthy.

In other words, the *cost* of maintaining our freedom is meeting our Responsibilities. Voluntarily. "Voluntary" here does not refer to donating our time and effort, although many people can, will, and do. But most churches pay their clergy and often their staff. Most organizations have employees. And of course in business, whether sole-proprietorship, partnership, or corporation, most everyone is paid.

What we have said that it is *so* preferable for voluntary governments to meet Responsibilities rather than Governments using force, for many reasons. We are talking about the voluntary groups of people such as churches, associations, unions, foundations, and corporations. Any group where being a member is voluntary, where people can choose to join or to leave. And where the group's government cannot use force against its members.

Here are some of the Responsibilities that must be met, if we are to stay free, as defined by our Rights:

The Right to <u>Life</u>. Our most basic and most precious Right. Which we also then have the Right to defend, both as individuals and as a nation. National defense is the one Responsibility that should always be administered at the highest level of national Government; however, recruitment of soldiers must remain voluntary. And the military must be used only for purposes which defend the lives of the citizens.

Beyond just defending our lives, though, we need to accept our Responsibility to ensure that our fellow citizens can *stay* alive, that they have the basic food, potable water, shelter, clothing, sewage systems, and health care necessary in order to survive. The benefits of accomplishing this through voluntary organizations cannot be overstated. Corporations in particular have shirked their duties in this regard. And as a result, we have inefficient, ineffective, bloated, redundant Government bureaucracies that implement upside-down solutions at enormous costs to both our pocketbooks and to our freedoms, without ever achieving our goals.

The Right to <u>Liberty</u>. Our Liberties include Freedom of Religion; Freedom of Speech; Freedom of the Press; Freedom to Assemble; Freedom to Join; and the Freedom to Communicate and express ourselves.

Each of these also applies in the negative; that is, for example, we have a Right to join whatever church we choose, but we also then have an equal Right *not* to join. We have a Right to speak, but we also have the Right *not* to speak.

Because every one of us has these Rights, then each of us simultaneously receives the Responsibility to honor the same Rights of our neighbors. This is where it can get tough, where we can easily destroy Liberty for everyone. Some examples: I have a Right to speak my mind, but at the same time you have a Right *not* to listen; you have a Right to choose *not* to hear my message, or be forced to listen to me. Similarly, I have a Right to my own religious beliefs and thus my own definition of morality, but at the same time you have a Right to yours, which may be entirely different; you have a Right to choose *not* to follow my definition of morality, or be forced to act as I see fit.

Tricky to balance sometimes. But the bottom line is that our freedoms stop at the point where they are interfering with another person's same freedoms.

This also applies to another Right that falls under the heading of Liberty, the Right to Privacy. This includes freedom from unwarranted search and from prying into our personal lives, especially by Governments. And when we allow the busybodies to pass laws against what consenting adults do in the privacy of their own homes, when their actions hurt no one but themselves, then all of the freedoms of the entire society are at risk, we are sliding down that slippery slope.

The Right to our <u>Pursuit of Happiness</u>. Because each person's happiness can only be determined by himself or herself, and because each of us has a Right to seek, to search for, our own happiness, then it follows that each of us is free to do as we please, so long as we are not hurting anyone else or interfering with their freedom to do as they please. You may recognize this as a different way of stating the Golden Rule.

Many of the Rights necessary to our Pursuit of Happiness are embodied in the Liberties we just discussed, Freedom of Speech and the Freedom to Join for example. People often refer to these liberties under the broad headings of human rights or civil rights. But there is an equally important set of Rights, without which we cannot pursue or find our happiness . . .

Private Property Rights are essential to a free and prosperous society. While economic rights are often thought of, or categorized, as separate from civil rights, they are in fact Siamese twins, two facets of the same diamond. Freedom of choice in both personal actions and economic decisions are essential to a free society.

There are four aspects of Personal Property Rights: (1) the Right to hold and use property; (2) the Right to sell, trade, rent, or give away the property, or not; (3) the Right to profit from the property, and to risk the property in seeking profits; and, (4) the Right to Contract, under agreements voluntarily entered into, enforceable under the law.

While most people agree with these concepts, they often fail to understand that the effect of these actions, freely undertaken, is free trade, free enterprise, and capitalism. These are just natural extensions of Personal Property Rights. And the result, through the "magic of markets" (win-win trades) and increased productivity, is real, honest progress toward prosperity. Every barrier to the free exercise of Private Property Rights inhibits real economic growth and true prosperity.

Do not misunderstand – when someone is hurting another through their activities, then it is the role and the obligation of Government to intervene, to protect the Rights of the other person. And Government may often need to referee when costs of economic actions are being borne by others without their consent, perhaps even without their knowledge.

But Government has some serious obligations in terms of protecting Private Property Rights. Government must guard against unlawful seizure. Government must resist the temptation to manipulate or fix prices. Government must avoid creating or allowing Monopolies. Government must ensure a sound and stable system of money in order for trades and Contracts to have validity. Government must never Inflate the money supply. Government must operate from balanced budgets and avoid debt. Government must practice the same sound, honest and transparent accounting that it expects of the citizens and market participants. And because people have the Right to risk their property and profit from it, Government must also allow them to fail. Government is the referee, not the player.

In a free society, Government's only Responsibility is to protect our Rights and Liberties. But our Responsibilities, as citizens of a free, democratic country, are to make sure that the Government itself is not violating our Rights; to educate ourselves as to how freedom works; to vote for folks that will follow the Constitution and the American Principles; to amend the Constitution when necessary; and to ensure that we do not allow the floodgates of tyranny to open. And to respect and honor the fact that every other citizen, everywhere, has the same Rights we that we do. They were born with them, just like you and me.

- - FPP - -

Chapter 18. you got no rights II

We discussed at length, in earlier chapters, the Principle that individuals have natural, unalienable Rights. We just described some of the Responsibilities that accompany those Rights.

Now let us ask these questions: if your Right is *yours,* can someone else own it? If your Right to Life is unalienable, can anyone take it away from you? If you have a natural Right to Freedom of Speech, can you give that Right away?

"No", of course, is the answer to each of those questions. Rights reside in the individual and cannot be taken or given away. (You may choose not to exercise your Freedom of Speech, but in doing so, you do not give up your Right to make a different choice at a different time.)

Responsibilities are another matter. We can, and often do, let other people take over our personal Responsibilities; and we can give them away, or employ others to meet them.

The point is an important one. Perhaps the most critical in this book. In a free country, in a democracy of, by, and for the people, in a society that recognizes unalienable individual Rights, the *Government has no Rights*, only Responsibilities.

The Government cannot, by definition, accept or take Rights that reside only in individuals. But what the Government can do is accept the Responsibilities that the people choose to have their Government assume ("by the people"). Thus the Government is a *servant* of the people, using its Force to execute those Responsibilities, on their behalf ("for the people"). And, of course, those who Govern are elected from among the citizens, "of the people".

This bears repeating: in a free country, Government has no Rights, only Responsibilities.

Lost American Principles: the Counter-revolution

Thus a letter like this, a "resolution", might be appropriate:

To President Obama, to the Justices of the Supreme Court, and to the 535 members of Congress:

> You, while serving in your capacity as Federal Officials of the Republic of the United States of America, have no rights, only Responsibilities, and those are to the people of America. First and foremost among your obligations is to defend and protect the individual Rights that each of us are entitled to.
>
> You have sworn to uphold the Constitution and we expect you to stop breaking that promise. If we are to have a Rule of Law in America, then that contract has to be the ultimate authority. Not you. Your role is to enforce the Rule of Law, like a referee.
>
> And we want you to remember that in your role as referee - - defending against majorities who would violate the Rights of minorities; and, constraining the twins of democracy and capitalism when they breach individual Rights - - in that role, you must remember that when the referee takes the side of one team rather than just enforcing the rules, or when the referee becomes a player, then the game is really over.
>
> In a free country, of the people, by the people, and for the people, committed to living under the Rule of Law rather than the laws of rulers, the Government has no rights, only Responsibilities.

Sincerely,

The citizens of America

- - FPP - -

Chapter 19. Guiding Principles for Government

If the goals are freedom, peace, and prosperity:

1. All people, everywhere, are created equal. Each and every individual has natural, equal, unalienable rights, regardless of race, color, creed, gender, nationality, or any other classification.

2. Those rights include: the Right to Life, and to Live; personal Liberties; and freedom of choice in each person's Pursuit of Happiness. Every Right also defines its accompanying Responsibilities; they are two side of the same coin.

3. Each individual's freedom to choose stops at the point where such a choice would interfere with, or violate, another person's rights. The basic moral principle is the Golden Rule.

4. In a free country, Government has no rights, only responsibilities. The two primary responsibilities of Government are the protection of individual Rights and the national defense.

5. Government must follow the Rule of Law, so that the people are not subjected to the laws of rulers. This is done through a Constitution that defines that Government's responsibilities; that itemizes individual Rights; and that specifies the structure of, and the limits of, the Government.

6. To establish Government, and maintain it, democracy is necessary, of the people, by the people, and for the people. Not as the structure of the Government, but as the means to establish the Rule of Law and then elect the officials of the Government.

7. In a democracy, Government cannot establish "sub-Governments" or agencies or bureaucracies which are not accountable to the people that are not subject to direct Congres-

Lost American Principles: the Counter-revolution

sional oversight. To empower such entities, and give them the ability to use deadly force, is to create little dictatorships in the midst of the country.

8. Ends do not necessarily justify means. The goals, no matter how desirable, can never justify the tactics, if they violate individual Rights. Governments, in gray areas, must always err on the side of individual Rights.

9. In the end, Governments are composed of people. Regular, fallible, flawed people. Granting them the honor of governing does not change that. In a democracy, then, the citizens must be ever-vigilant, for their elected officials will always have negative impulses and will often make mistakes; it is the patriotic duty of the people to protect ourselves and their freedoms.

10. Voluntary governments are preferable to Government in meeting responsibilities. The Government must allow and encourage voluntary solutions, using its force only as a last resort, only when responsibilities are not otherwise being met. The Government must not use its force to "partner" with voluntary organizations. And if the Government has, by necessity, used force to meet certain responsibilities, it must extract itself by encouraging and allowing voluntary solutions, or solutions at lower levels of Government, at the first opportunity.

- - FPP - -

Chapter 20. Close Encounter in the Woods

A long, long time ago, Tnuh was doing what she always did, gathering fruits and nuts in the hills. She was an experienced gatherer.

And at the river, Hsif was doing what he always did: fishing. He was a good and knowledgeable fisherman.

One day, as they were returning home, their paths crossed in the woods. Tnuh studied the little man with his stringer of fish and she imagined spearing him and taking his fish.

Hsif eyed the woman and her basket of fruit, and envisioned himself clubbing her and taking the fruit home to his family.

Tnuh broke the silence; she said "You seem to have plenty of fish. Would you trade for some of my fruit?"

Hsif considered for a moment, and then he replied, "I will give you four fish for three of your melons."

Hsif said that was too high a price and offered two of her melons for four fish. They agreed. They traded. And they both hurried home to share the good news - - and their bounty of rare treats - - with their families.

Look – I did not want to tell you ahead of time that we were going to study economics, because I know how most folks feel about the subject. But there you have it. If you understand the little story above, and its implications, you have just completed the first course in economics, Economics 101.

Here are the lessons:

1. <u>Free Trade</u> is simply people *voluntarily* exchanging their property. Or not.

2. Both Tnuh and Hsif were better off by trading. Because after the trade, Tnuh had fish she wanted more than melons. And Hsif had melons he valued more than his fish. That is called the <u>Magic of the Market</u>, because *both* families now had more than they started with, had increased their wealth, from their stand-

point. This is called a win-win, which can only occur when trade is free.

3. The two traders discussed the amounts of goods for which they were willing to trade, at that particular moment, in that particular place, under those circumstances. The price. Which is nothing more than the *communication* of the amounts one would consider trading for. First they communicated little "p" prices, which are the offers and bids that neither would agree to. In other words, Hsif could set any price he wanted, even a very high one. But if Tnuh is free *not* to accept that price, and so chooses, then it is nothing more than a wish on Hsif's part.

But once they agreed to the trade, the big "P" Price was established, which is communicated as the amount of goods each agreed to trade. (The Price of a melon was two fish. The Price of a fish was one-half of a melon.) Prices are a form of communication, the free speech required for personal property Rights, the language of free markets. And the way that we measure trades.

4. Had Tnuh not been able to find melons, she would have had nothing to trade. Her productivity is what allowed her to enrich herself further, through the Magic of the Market, by trading. Same with Hsif.

5. And finally, they understood that it was better to trade than to kill the other person for their bounty. Tnuh knew nothing about fishing, and Hsif was a poor gatherer. It was their specialization that allowed them to be more productive. Had Tnuh speared the little man, she would have gained a few fish; but only once. She would have given up the opportunity to obtain more fish later on, had she eliminated the fisherman.

Free trade; the Magic of the Market; offers, bids and Prices; productivity; and specialization. These are the elements of Free Markets, or Free Enterprise. Remember this story when the "Complexinators" try to baffle you with BS. (Complexinators try to tell us that these things are *so complex* today; that simple truths no longer work; that everything is different; and that their otherwise-implausible solutions will somehow solve the complexity.)

Consider the brick. It is very simple, just dried mud and straw. But lots of simple bricks, built one upon another, can produce a huge, sprawling castle, with countless rooms and corridors and dungeons. So don't let the Complexinators convince you that because the building is "complex", because it is hard to even know of all of its various rooms and hidden places, that the bricks no longer mean anything, that we can destroy the bricks in order to save the castle.

Like a castle made of bricks, everything in the economy, no matter how big, is built upon these same little trades. And when we destroy the freedom to trade, the basic building blocks, we damage the economy, perhaps even destroy it.

What destroys the building bricks of an economy? Price controls; interest manipulation; Monopolies; fiat money; Inflation; and excessive credit (debt), to name a few. Laws that *require* you to trade, when you would not otherwise have done so or laws that do not allow free trade. Censorship of, or fixing, prices; free prices are as essential to freedom as free presses. In other words, if we believe in liberty and in Private Property, then free trade is simply a Right. And free markets result.

A place for Government? Of course. Remember, their job is to protect our Rights. So Government must ensure that one trader is not violating the Rights of others. Government must defend and protect Private Property Rights and contracts and voluntary trade, establish and enforce the rules of fair play, like a referee. Protect the Right to profit. Defend the Right to fail. Virtually every major economic challenge that we are facing today can be traced directly to Government's inability, or unwillingness, to do these things, to meet their sworn responsibilities to us.

- - FPP - -

21. What's that in your pocket? *A chicken??*

Some centuries later, the descendants of Tnuh and Hsif were raising poultry and livestock, producing goods. The barter and trading had expanded. The free markets were working. But folks encountered a problem. The fellow with the chickens wanted some apples. But the apple gal did not want chickens, she wanted wheat. And the wheat grower wanted a pair of boots. And so on. It was becoming hard to trade.

So they called a town meeting to address the issue. Someone said, "Well why don't we use *money*?" Another asked, "What is money? And where would it come from?"

"If we all agree to use a certain commodity," was the answer, "if we all agree to accept it in trade, then that commodity would become our money. That would make trading much easier; when we accept the "money" for our goods, then we can use it to trade for the things we want."

Everyone agreed that they needed to adopt something as their money; it would benefit everyone if a suitable commodity could be found. So different people took turns making a pitch for their "commodity" to become the official money.

First was the chicken fellow. He said, "everyone loves chickens" and explained their versatility; they could be eaten, or provide eggs. Plus, the live chickens control the populations of bugs and insects. Someone asked, "If we make chickens money, will that include little chickens and big chickens? Bantams and Leghorns? Roosters and hens? Couldn't there be large differences between individual chickens?" The chicken fellow explained, "All money will be chickens, but not all chickens will be money. We will decide on a standard."

After some discussion, that idea was voted down. Partly because of the problem of variation in individual chickens, but also because people felt that packing chickens around in their pocket would be inconvenient. And messy. ("what's *that?*")

Then the apple gal made her case. Unlike chickens, she said, her apples were pretty uniform and easy to carry. Again she made the point that all money would be apples, but not all apples would be money. She proposed that Red Delicious apples become the official money. The people rejected that idea,

What's that in your pocket? A chicken??

too. Not only do apples spoil easily, making them hard to store or save, but one bad apple could ruin the whole basket.

Someone suggested that they just use the leaves of trees for money. But they realized that they are too abundant, that it could take wheelbarrows full of leaves to buy anything. Leaves simply did not have any real value in and of themselves; they were not a commodity. And the leaf supply would be subject to huge fluctuations, constantly changing the buying power of the money, and making the marketplace unstable, to say the least.

They realized that they needed to choose something that had real value, before it could be used as money. They knew that it must not spoil or rot. They understood that it should be easy to carry and convenient for making trades. And they agreed that each unit must be identical to the next. And when the cattleman made his pitch, for cows as money, they thought about the difficulty of trading a cow for a bag of apples. So they reasoned that the commodity must be something that is easily divided into smaller parts.

When Mr. Aurum, the old miner, finally proposed to make gold the official money, the people realized that gold was the only viable solution. He explained that gold was virtually indestructible, not subject to spoiling or rotting. That it was in sufficient supply to function as money, but still rare enough to be very valuable. Gold is a valuable commodity in and of itself, and has many uses, from industrial applications to jewelry. It is easily minted into coins of various denominations, large and small, and the gold coins are easily carried and stored. They knew they had found their money.

The miner continued, "All money will be gold, but not all gold will be money. We will agree on the sizes, the amount of gold in each coin. The coins will be stamped with their certified gold content, and those standards will be strictly enforced. Thus everyone will be assured that the coins are real and that they contain the amount of gold that is specified on their face. We will not attempt to regulate the price of the coins, or to impose a specific value, because only you, the folks doing the trading, know what you are willing to trade your coins for."

The miner went a step further, "Because I have the mine and a supply of gold, and because I have access to a minting machine, you should grant me the exclusive rights to mint the money for you. That way I can protect your money supply."

At first everyone thought that sounded fine. Until someone said, "Wait a minute. Are we suggesting that we give Mr. Aurum a Monopoly on the minting of our coins? Won't that be a conflict of interest? And wouldn't that allow him to manipulate the quantity and value of our money?"

After the people thought it through, they decided that the way to ensure a safe, stable money system was to allow for as many "authorized" minters of coins as wanted to participate. And to keep the minting operations completely separate from the mining and from the markets for raw gold and jewelry. That way, the value of the gold coins, the Money, would always be "regulated" and held in check by the value of gold bullion; if coins became too abundant and dropped in value, folks would exchange them for bullion and fewer would be minted. On the other hand, if gold coins were in short supply, and the price was rising, the mints would rush to produce more coins.

And so our little band of free traders discovered what history has proven over and over: there is no known substitute for money made of precious metals. It is the best system for providing a stable money supply, preventing huge fluctuations and Inflations, and for building true economic prosperity.

The very worst idea, of course, was declaring tree leaves to be money. Which is, in effect, what we do today. Of course the Federal Reserve owns the only tree (an enormous one). And they stamp the leaves with their imprint. But it is still just pieces of paper, the quantities determined at the whims of the central bank. Federal Reserve Notes are hardly a commodity. And their only value is that we are required *by law* to accept them . . . perhaps it is time to insist upon real money again?

- - FPP - -

Chapter 22. The Coin Warehouse

Warehouses have long been used by farmers to store their crops. When Jones deposits his wheat in the warehouse, the warehouse gives him a receipt. And when Jones wants his wheat back, he trades his receipt for the wheat. (Or, in the meantime, he might sell his receipt to someone else, who could then retrieve the wheat.) The warehouses charge a fee for this service, of course.

After the town folk officially sanctioned gold coins as their money, and when folks started to accumulate more coins than they wanted to pack around, they looked for a safe place to keep them. And some enterprising people set up little warehouses for money, where people could "bank" their gold. Banks. For a fee, the bankers stored the money and issued a receipt. And when folks wanted to retrieve their coins, they redeemed their receipts for the coins; they could "demand" their deposited money. (Thus the name, "demand deposits".)

But the bankers got greedy. Seeing all these coins stacked in their warehouse, sitting there idle when they could be loaned out for interest . . . well, it was just too much temptation. You see, not everyone demanded their coins at the same time, so there was, in effect, a supply of money that was not being used. Not the bankers' money, mind you, but still unused.

So the bankers determined that if they could keep enough on hand, in "reserve", to meet the day-to-day demands, then they could loan out all of the rest of the coins, for interest, and no one would be the wiser. So they lent away. They got the credit flowing, as they say. The trick, of course, was not to reveal the scam; if the folks realized that there was not enough money in the bank to give them their money back, then they might panic. And the bank would be busted.

Was fifty percent enough to hold in reserve, while loaning out the other half? Forty percent? You may know that they settled in, generally, on a range of about ten to twenty percent reserves, loaning out the rest of the folks' money. That worked for most of the banks, most of the time. Until twenty-one percent of the real owners showed up on the same day to demand their deposits. Then the gig was up. There wasn't enough money.

Lost American Principles: the Counter-revolution

They called that a "run on the bank", and they usually blamed the citizens themselves for their panicky behavior. But in truth *the bank was already insolvent*. It never kept all the money in the warehouse; it never had enough to meet all of the demands it had promised. The scam had simply been revealed.

That is called "fractional reserve" banking. The banks, while saying you have a "demand deposit" (in your checking and savings accounts), do not keep your money in their safes. They lend out all but a small reserve, a fraction of the deposits. This scam was invented in the 1700's and is institutionalized today.

Fractional reserve banking seems to be an obvious violation of personal property Rights (the right to profit from what you own); is undoubtedly immoral; and should be illegal. Instead, our Government has seen fit not only to condone the practice, but to encourage it. In fact, due to some twisted court rulings, in America today the law says that the money you deposit in your checking and savings accounts is no longer yours; it becomes the property of the bank! The banks give you an IOU, of course, and they should pay it back, but it becomes "theirs" to invest as they wish, and to profit from.

And profit they do. Because on the surface it would seem that if you deposit $10,000, and if the bank is required to keep ten percent in reserve, then the bank could only loan out $9,000. But the real effect is that within a short time your $10,000 becomes the reserve for $100,000 in loans. Check it out: the banker tells you that he pays you three percent interest and then only gets six percent when he loans it out (implying that he only has a gross profit of three percent). But in reality, he is paying three percent to you on your ten thousand, ($300 per year) while collecting six percent on the one-hundred thousand in loans he is making using your money as the reserve ($6,000 per year).

[*footnote: It gets worse. Fractional reserves are today often closer to five percent. (The bank can loan out $200,000 against your $10,000.) They can even "buy" deposits from the Monopoly central bank, in order to ratchet up their leverage even further. The Monopoly central bank, the Fed, simply creates these "reserves" out of thin air . . .]

The Coin Warehouse

    For whatever reasons, fractional reserve banking has been allowed for the last couple of centuries, in spite of the constant stream of bank runs and bank failures that occurred whenever the insolvencies were revealed. Rather than eliminate the immoral practice, we actually put in place a Monopoly national bank to backstop and promote it: in 1913, with the formation of the Federal Reserve (not part of our Government), fractional reserve banking became institutionalized. And the bankers received the Government seal of approval.

Go back, for a moment, to your $10,000 deposit. You now know that the bank makes $100,000 in loans, or more, against your deposit. But where does the other $90,000 come from, the money that they are loaning out? Simple. They just make a computer entry into the account of the borrowers. *The banks create electronic "money" out of thin air.* So whenever "credit is flowing", the money supply is being Inflated. And Inflation causes prices to rise, distorts markets, creates bubbles, and taxes the poor and middle classes.
    And, conversely, whenever credit stops flowing, when people feel like maybe they don't need or want any more debt, then the money supply deflates, causing lower prices and economic contractions. Like now.

It's bad enough that we allow the unethical practice of fractional reserves, letting banks profit enormously from *our* private property, permitting them to operate in a constant state of insolvency. But the Inflation of the money supply that follows wreaks even more havoc. Inflation, the silent, deadly killer of economies, is not understood by most folks. Or, apparently, by politicians.

- - FPP - -

Chapter 23. Old Blue, the Ugly Horse

In a far corner of the countryside, a young family carved a home out of the wilderness. They cleared the land, built a cabin with the trees, uprooted the stumps, and tilled the soil by hand with a crude plow. They were barely able to survive, struggling through several harsh seasons. Eventually, though, they were able to grow more food than they needed for themselves.

They traded their extra apples for the gold coins that had been agreed to as money. And then traded the coins for other things, little extras, an occasional luxury. But Ma was wise. Rather than spend all of the coins on dresses and candy, she always put a few in the cookie jar, in savings. Then one day, Ma and Pa took their saved coins and bought a horse to pull the plow. They couldn't afford much, so they bought Old Blue, an ugly old nag that no self-respecting equestran would ride, but a big strong horse nonetheless.

With the additional horse power, they were able to clear and maintain twice the amount of land. And their apple crops increased exponentially. They traded the apples for more coins, some of which they traded for other things - - consumed - - and some of which went into the cookie jar.

The process repeated when Ma and Pa decided to buy a tractor. They knew it was risky, that it would take lots of apples to maintain the expensive tractor. But they were willing to take the risk. They knew they might fail, perhaps even lose their little farm; there was a real chance that they might go broke and have to start all over again. But they also thought they had an opportunity for even greater rewards, so they were willing to take the risk. And they made that choice.

And that's our second course in economics, Economics 102.

Here are the key points:

1. Savings, the coins in the cookie jar that were not used right away for <u>consumption</u>, will eventually be used in one of two ways. They might be used for consumption at a later date, like

when an emergency arises, or when Mary needs a wedding dress. Or, the coins can be invested into tools that will increase production; if used this way, those savings are capital, or the source of capital (versus consumption).

2. Tools increase productivity. Just as a lever enables a man to move a much larger rock, tools enable people to produce more. The plow was a great tool, and became even more effective when Old Blue pulled it.

3. Bigger, better tools require capital investments. (Always remember that savings are the source of these capital investments.) Like the tractor.

4. Investments require risk. Entrepreneurs and investors risk capital. They must do so voluntarily, if they are to receive the rewards. And they must be free to fail; they must bear the risk that justifies the rewards. If they are not free to fail, then it is not risk. If they are not free to fail, the profits are not justified. If they are not free to fail, they are not free.

5. Ma and Pa will have many expenses: fuel and maintenance; insurance; seedlings; fertilizer . . . the list is long. And these must be paid. But if they are eventually able to sell their crop for an amount more than these expenses, that is their profit. And, being that they are putting their entire farm at risk, they are entitled to all of the profits they can muster.

6. Capital, derived from savings, invested in tools, in hopes of making a profit, but with the real risk of failure - that's what Ma and Pa were up to. And there is a word for that: Capitalism. For goodness sakes, Ma and Pa were Capitalists!

Capitalism is nothing more, nothing less, than people freely exercising their private property rights (to hold and use; to profit from; to trade; and to contract). Capitalists choose to risk their private property in order to profit.

Not only does this increase productivity, but it also increases wealth as the products work their magic in free markets.

Lost American Principles: the Counter-revolution

And it encourages the development of even more and better tools, more savings, more investment. Capitalism in a free enterprise system creates a wonderful upward spiral.

Marx argued against this, of course. But remember, Marx (and the socialists) did not believe in private property in the first place, or any other natural rights. As we have seen, free trade and free markets were natural and beneficial for Tnuh and Hsif. And capitalism seemed natural for Ma and Pa. Free trade, free markets, and capitalism are natural - - "all natural" as the ads say - - because they flow from the natural Rights and Liberties that we discussed in earlier chapters.

Again, don't let the Complexinators trick you. The freedom to risk one's capital is one of the cornerstones of economies. When you start destroying those, regardless of the motive, the building is going to sag, and eventually crumble.

Capitalists often have an urge to violate people's Rights in their quest for profits. Just as majorities have the urge to abuse the Rights of minorities. While both democracy and capitalism are dynamic and healthy and vital - - they are the very best way to achieve our goals as a society - - they still need a referee to ensure that everyone is playing fair, to constrain them when individual citizens are being hurt rather than benefiting.

But make no mistake: capitalism is no more a bad thing than is democracy. Both are essential to our goals.

- - FPP - -

Chapter 24. Smokey the Bear

Do you remember Smokey? I grew up with him (showing my age, yes?) and I still remember the song on the radio:

> "Smokey the Bear, Smokey the Bear,
> Howlin' and a growlin' and a sniffin' the air
> He can find a fire, before it starts to flame,
> That's why they call him Smokey, that's how he got his name."
>
> Followed by Smokey saying, "Only you can prevent forest fires".

At least that's my recollection. Along with the words "Don't be a guberif" painted in large letters on the highways (firebug backwards).

Smokey Bear, a Symbol used by the US Forest Service, was "born" in 1944. Smokey reinforced the goal of the Forest Service to "stomp out forest fires". And for many decades, the Forest Service, in cooperation with many other agencies, spent vast resources, billions of dollars and millions of man hours, even lost lives, to stomp out every forest fire, as quickly as possible, wherever it occurred.

Then, in 1988, during drought conditions, the Yellowstone fires broke out. Televisions, magazines and newspapers all showed the terrible destruction of Yellowstone National Park. It looked like a bombed-out war zone, and many mourned the death and destruction of one of our great national treasures.

Just a few years later, though, we began to see photos of large tracts of green in the Park, sleek animals, and more of them. Time would show that these fires were actually healthy for the Park. And that the fire was inevitable.

In the ensuing analysis, more folks began to acknowledge that fires were a *natural* part of the ecology, that fire cleaned out weak and failing plants, and removed the accumulations of dead grass and branches and leaves and trees. In the absence of fire, these highly flammable fuels build up, crowding

Lost American Principles: the Counter-revolution

out young plants and accumulating to the point where they actually sicken the forest. The longer natural fires are prevented, the more buildup. Until the inevitable dry season, when a fire breaks out and cannot be controlled; there is simply too much volatile fuel. And then the fires burn much larger, longer and hotter, causing immeasurably more damage than the smaller fires would have.

Today, the policy is more often to let naturally occurring wildfires burn, as long as they do not threaten lives or private property. This produces much healthier, more natural forests, as well as more food and better habitat for the wild inhabitants of the forest. Stated another way, occasional wildfires are part of nature, and healthy for the ecology of the forests.

We can hardly wait for the day when it dawns on folks that our economy works much the same way. When businesses are weak or dead, the fires of bankruptcy and liquidation clean them out and create more opportunity and better conditions for the healthier inhabitants of the economy. And if we "stomp out" bankruptcy, if we allow failed businesses to remain by bailing them out, then the buildup of volatile enterprises will eventually reach a flash point. And we will feel the heat of the meltdown.

So we are at an important crossroads. While we have generally understood this principle in the past, we are now embarking on an unprecedented attempt to violate nature.

Look - the weather naturally cycles. We go from a series of warm summers to years of unusual cold, from wet years to drought. And economies cycle naturally, as well. They heat up and then cool, they experience sunny days and storms. Governments can no more control the recessions and the prosperity in economies than they can control the summer temperatures and rainfall in Yellowstone Park.

We are now in an economic drought, a cool-down, a severe storm, a recession, if not a depression. And the weak and dead businesses are burning down. That leaves us in a bit of a quandary: should we let them burn (using bankruptcy, the orderly process to liquidate them at the least cost) or should we try to prop them up, bail them out, keep them going.

Smokey the Bear

Most Americans probably understand that bankruptcy is the best option for failed businesses. In 2002, a huge company called WorldCom, Inc., after committing the largest corporate fraud in history, also became the largest bankruptcy in US history. The bankruptcy judge appointed Richard Breeden to oversee the liquidation and he managed to keep 60,000 of the company's 75,000 employees on the payroll and delivered $12 Billion dollars to the company's creditors. When the company emerged from bankruptcy protection, it was eventually combined into MCI, Inc, now part of Verizon Communications.

But suddenly last Fall, we were told that we can no longer do this, that if we didn't act immediately to bail out companies like Bear Stearns and AIG we would suffer dire consequences. (Many call that the "politics of fear" . . . makes you question motivations. And who was really being protected? Obviously not us.) An eager Congress, encouraged by the Bush folks, rushed to spend $700 Billion of our money for bailouts. (Mr. Breeden contends that under bankruptcy, AIG could have sold all of its profitable divisions and then liquidated the part of the company that was holding those toxic assets.) But the politicians bailed away. On our dime.

And then, disappointingly, President Obama picked right up where the last Administration left off. Well, that's not quite correct, because Obama, his cabinet members, and the new Congress are *accelerating* the Bush policies. Not exactly the change we were promised.

We have since passed another $800 Billion or so in bailout legislation, in addition to other substantial commitments and government guarantees (guaranteed by our wallets, of course). On top of that, we are now in the process of racking up probably at least a $2 Trillion dollar budget shortfall this year, likely closer to $3 Trillion, nearly a quarter of our national annual production (GDP), if we do not make an abrupt change in direction.

Look at what has happened: AIG has been back to the trough repeatedly. First we gave them $85 Billion, but when that wasn't enough, we gave them more. And more. The total is about $170 Billion as I write, with no guarantee that will keep

Lost American Principles: the Counter-revolution

them afloat. And no one will even disclose where that money is going.

Same with the automakers. In fact, after the automakers received their injections (of our cash), then their *suppliers* asked for support (which we gave). Now the auto *dealers* want help. Where does it stop? The folks who provide rubber to the tire makers, and then the businesses that supply the rubber makers? The folks that install GPS and stereos in new cars, and then the GPS manufacturers? Eventually, it leads to every business in the economy. So in effect, we are letting the politicos in Washington DC decide who lives and who dies in the economy. Instead of the marketplace, where we cast *our* votes.

And even if it somehow made sense to fight this fire, how can anyone think that we have enough resources to put it out? This is big. The fuel buildup is enormous. Like Yellowstone, it is not just one fire, but a number of smaller fires, all raging at the same time. Look - we have the tools to limit damages, through the bankruptcy courts. And administering and working through these multiple large bankruptcies would take all of our efforts and energy.

Instead, we are exhausting all of our resources, and indebting our kids and grandkids, in a vain attempt to extinguish all of the fires. We couldn't do it at Yellowstone. And we can't do it now. Besides, even if we did succeed, what is the result? Enormous piles of unburned deadwood, ready at the first little lightning strike to burst into an even larger, more-destructive fire.

But another side of the story is reflected in today's Forest Service policy of letting wildfires burn as long as they do not threaten lives or property. In our current economic crisis, are lives and property threatened? Does that demand "action"?

Well this is not an ordinary wildfire, this is a Yellowstone. We have to realize that Smokey simply will not be able to stomp it out. Yes, there is going to be property damage. We are already seeing it; people are losing their homes and possessions, for goodness sake. The best we can do is prevent the loss of life, and work around the edges. This thing has to burn itself out. And we are all going to have to pull together in the wake

Smokey the Bear

of its destruction. In the wake of the deep recession, probably depression.

And perhaps we ought to pull a majority of us together and send along this letter:

Mr. President, Senators, and Representatives,

Please listen to us. Take a deep breath and use some common sense. You have to think about what is best for America in the long run, not just for tomorrow's press conference, not just for the next few months, not just for the next election. Most of us are ready to endure the pain; for goodness sakes, we are *already* paying the price. If it gets worse before it gets better, so be it; it's time for all of us to bear the responsibility for our foolishness and our false prosperity. To leave our kids and grandkids with an even worse mess, to make things a little more comfortable for ourselves now, knowing the inevitable pain we are laying off on them, is simply not right. It is not honest. It is not fair. It is not what America was supposed to be about.

Have you not considered the consequences for our children? And their kids? Or do you somehow truly believe that we can flaunt the natural laws of economics without consequence? Perhaps you believe that *your* kids will be able to avoid what our kids will have to endure. We don't know your "whys", we only know that the actions being taken by our Government are hurling us headlong down the path to disaster. Sooner or later. A large disaster now, to be sure, but an enormous conflagration later, if we put it off.

The economy has been mismanaged for decades and these fires need to burn. Look - we can get through this. Your throwing our money at the problems shows a complete lack of trust in the American people; you act as if only *you* can spend our money in a way that will produce a viable economy. And as if only *you* can provide for us, keep us safe, give us jobs. That is simply not true. We are strong and resilient and industrious. We are caring and we will help one another through this depression. Most of us would rather just get it over with than pawn it off on our grandkids.

Lost American Principles: the Counter-revolution

And it is an insult to us that you can rationalize ("rational lies") that it is somehow OK to hand our money to businesses that have raked in billions of dollars and now find themselves in trouble. That giving them our money "protects" us. (In the same way that a shopkeeper is forced to hand over money to the mafia thug for "protection'?) And it is a slap in the face to the people who pay their bills and pay their mortgages when you use their money to bailout folks who do not pay, or should never have received a loan in the first place.

Stop the madness. Stop the bailouts. Stop spending our money. Stop deficit spending. Let the deadwood burn; let failing businesses fail. Start balancing the budget and reducing our debt. Yes, *of course that will make things "worse"*. For a while. We know that. We can deal with the truth. But that does not mean that you "need to act". Because in a few short years, like Yellowstone, we will then see the green pastures returning and a far stronger, healthier economy emerging.

That's what you should be telling us, that working our way through this depression in an honest and responsible way will bring the dawn of a better day. While it will be hard, and painful, it is the best alternative, because bailouts and deficits and more credit (debt) will only prolong the inevitable.

In the mean time, if we can but learn from this crisis, we can go to work on the systemic causes of the boom and bust cycles, like the intentional Inflation of the money supply which breeds unhealthy ventures, and produces false prosperity and excessive buildups of volatile enterprise. Then we will be able to deal with the smaller wildfires that occur in the dry years.

Smokey Bear said, "Don't be a guberif". We say to you, "Don't be a tnaryt".

- - FPP - -

Chapter 25. Too Big to Fail

Let me get this straight: if a business is not profitable, it goes out of business. And we know, over the long run, that is good for the greater economy, because the business was wasting resources. So when a small company is spending more than it is producing - - when it is losing money - - it goes bankrupt, but it has only wasted a small amount of resources.

When a large company is losing money, it becomes even more important that it has the freedom to fail, because it is wasting a large amount of resources.

But when an enormous company is failing, even though it is obviously wasting enormous amounts of resources, we are obliged to take hard-earned money from our wallets and hand it to over to them. Actually help them waste enormous amounts of our country's resources? In hopes that they might not waste more? What? Tell me I am not hearing this correctly. That sounds like a huge risk, a risk that ought to be reserved to wealthy, sophisticated investors, not an "investment" that our own Government would force us to make.

"Oh," they say, "but they are too big to fail. If that company fails, the entire economy will suffer. We must act quickly in order to protect Main Street".

Do they think we are stupid? (Well, on second thought, maybe we are; we let them do it.) But this too-big-to-fail argument is greatly flawed, on so many levels:

First, the market has a mechanism to digest these failing entities; it is called bankruptcy. And all it does, essentially, is stop the bleeding; bankruptcy protection shelters the business from further losses (waste of resources) while the assets are liquidated and the business is restructured. In fact, businesses often come out of bankruptcy much stronger, acquired by people who are better at that business. In any case, this is an excellent and time-proven way to weed out the wasters and make room for more successful ventures. And the best way to minimize the damage to the greater economy. Bailouts, on the other hand, do not stop the bleeding; in fact, they enable more loss of blood.

Second, they say the economy will suffer. But the economy is *already* suffering, by definition. If the company is that big and is losing money, then it is sucking resources from the economy. And hurting the people within that economy. So forcing the very people who are being hurt by this company to send cash to that same company seems, well . . . "a moral hazard", in the politi-speak of the day. If we are doing it to keep the employees of that company on the payroll, then we are simply forcing others to pay their salaries. And if that is the case, we would all be better off if we put them to work in more productive endeavors. Besides, the bankruptcy process often keeps a large percentage of those folks employed.

Third, bailouts distort the markets, because if the market knows that the Government is going to come to the rescue, then that asset or entity becomes "safer", and thus commands a higher price than it should. This puts a lower relative value on better businesses and assets; in other words, the Government intervention actually encourages poor investments and displaces better investments that would grow the greater economy.

Fourth, these bailouts of multiple businesses, all "too big to fail", sound exactly like the actions of a person addicted to gambling. After a "bad string of losses", the gambler will often make ever larger, more foolish, desperate bets until he is completely broke. And our leaders seem hell-bent on breaking us. "For our own good", of course.

There is one possible justification for these bailouts that occurs to me: what if our Government knew that this economic crisis was planned or contrived somehow, by central banks and/or foreign countries, with the goal of buying up all of these enormous businesses at bargain-basement prices, when they go bankrupt. (Now there's a movie for you.) Now I'm not much on conspiracy theories and this seems a little far-fetched, but if it were true, I could see how our President and Congress might justify spending these otherwise unconscionable amounts of money to keep these businesses out of bankruptcy.

Maybe there really are some of those elements involved. Certainly the intentional Inflation of our fiat money supply has created an enormous credit bubble that is trying to deflate. And at the root of that problem is the real systemic risk, the Monopolies and central banks and the scary amount of wealth and power that they wield.

In the real world, in a real economy, no business is too big to fail. Quite the opposite; if a business is wasting resources, beyond just a seasonal slump or a one-time event, then the larger the business, the more important that it is free to fail. It seems like our leaders would know that. So we need to investigate their true motivation for these desperate, foolish acts. And their rush to incur debts the likes of which the world has never seen. If the real reason for these irrational actions is plain old political posturing, so that they can brag to the people back on Main Street that they "acted", so that they can hand out goodies in our times of need, so that they can get re-elected, God help us all.

Is *America* too big to fail? Hardly. The largest empires throughout history have always fallen. And usually when the empire got too large, when the spending and warring were simply no longer sustainable, even as they tried to inflate-away their debts. Are we going to repeat history, or are we going to insist on real change?

- - FPP - -

Chapter 26. Toxic Assets

If you look up the word "toxic", you will find meanings like harmful, malicious, and poisonous, harmful and debilitating. Look up "assets" and you will see them referred to as property owned, or the value of property owned. So how did our financial institutions come to own poisonous property? Was it just some accident of nature? A failure of the markets? What are these things and how did they come about?

Well, "toxic assets" is just a fancy word for stupid loans. And the derivatives that followed. These loans were made to people who were *very likely to default*. Which leads us to three questions: (1) why would anyone want to make these loans? (2) why did our regulators allow these loans to be made?; and, (3) does it even matter - if so, what should be done?

<u>First, why would anyone make stupid loans</u>? Short answer: windfall profits. But wait, if the bank makes a loan that is likely to fail, won't it *lose* money, rather than profit? Good question. And yes, in a free marketplace, it would. But they have perpetrated a scam, a "money-laundering" scheme, on a monumental scale. They found a way, supported at every step by our Government, to turn poison into gold.

William K. Black calls the current batch of failing loans "liars loans".* The mortgage bankers knowingly promoted loans to people who they *knew* were not qualified for the loans they were offered. In the trade, he says, some of these were referred to as "ninja loans" (No Income verification, No Job verification, no Asset verification). In fact, Mr. Black says that sometimes the bankers themselves, not just the borrowers, may have exaggerated incomes and assets.

Again, why? Well, the bankers were being pushed and encouraged - - and even required by law - - to make such loans, in order to fulfill the politicians' promises that everyone should and would own a home. The Government was even insuring many of these loans (with taxpayer dollars).

[* footnote: watch PBS's Bill Moyers interview of Mr. Black at www.pbs.org/moyers/journal/04032009/watch.html
Very worthwhile.]

Toxic Assets

At the same time, the bankers plotted a scam, elegant in its execution, sinister in its results. It required a conspiracy, of course, but the players were all too willing to cooperate; the money - - the vulgar amounts of money - - would buy all of the necessary players. And the regulators would be held at bay by the Government itself; after all, it was the Government promoting these "liars loans" in the first place. The scope of this makes Bernie Madoff look like a petty thief.

When a bank has a high-risk loan on its books, not only is it at risk of default, but because that loan is weak, this also reduces the bank's ability to "leverage", to make even more loans, against that asset. It is, in relation to the bank's potential profits, a "harmful" and "debilitating" asset on its books.

But if a hundred mortgages are bundled up together, as one asset package, then the risk is lessened somewhat, because they may not all default. So the banks sold "bundles" of these liars loans to the Wall Street bankers. The Wall Street bankers in turn sold pieces of these bundles ("securitized" bonds, or "derivatives", of the original mortgages). But, knowing that most folks would not want a bundle of poison any more than a single dose, they needed to "dress up" their bonds first.

So the Wall Street bankers turned to the Ratings Agencies, the people who rate bonds as to their risk. Of course, the bankers pay the agencies for these ratings, so they are suspect from the outset. But the agencies, realizing the profits to be made if they could produce favorable ratings, found economists to create wonderful econometric models, based on ethereal mathematical equations, to support the notion that these bundles of toxic assets were not risky. (Their convoluted theories go something like this: "based on extensive study of the last 25 years, we have seen no instance of large numbers of defaults, and our computer models prove that the probability that they might default now is probably low.")

Thus most of these bonds, pieces of bundles of toxic assets, were rated AAA. And according to *Investopedia.com*, "AAA bonds are thought to have *virtually no risk of default.*" Voila! From toxic assets to AAA bonds!

Lost American Principles: the Counter-revolution

Then Wall Street sold these "derivatives" to willing buyers worldwide, leveraging their own assets at margins of 30:1 (aka gambling), skimming windfall profits, and paying enormous bonuses in the process. Even that wasn't enough; they created even more derivatives out of the derivatives, such as the Credit Default Swaps.

Who do you suppose were among the biggest buyers of this repackaged poison? The Banks, of course.* What started out as toxic mortgages now appeared on their financials as AAA bonds, assets that they now could leverage, make more loans against, at a factor of 20 or 30.

When we finally "discovered" that these were not really AAA bonds, but were in fact liars loans (when the scam was revealed), the perpetrators found themselves not only insolvent, but way over-leveraged, unable to meet their obligations. The credit bubble began collapsing. And our Government rushed in to pump it back up, with bailouts and TARP funds and guarantees . . . trying frantically to rebuild "confidence" in the confidence game, attempting to keep the scheme afloat.

Second, why were those loans allowed to happen? As we said, the politicians had promised the citizens that a vote for them would mean home ownership for everyone. And so they encouraged (stupid) loans, mandated ("liars") loans, and insured ("ninja") loans. Pure politics. Otherwise there might have been more concern about incurring such risky debt.

But that is the tip of the iceberg; there is a deeper, darker "secret" as well. As I said, this is a scam on top of a fraud. You see, some decades back, our Government legalized fractional reserve banking, and then granted a monopoly to the national bank (the national bank is called the "Federal Reserve" but it is not part of our Government). Thus, working together, they have created the tools for Inflation of the money supply, *intentionally* eroding the buying power of our "dollars". This cozy relationship allows the banks to earn windfall profits - -

[*footnote: In America, just five huge Banks own something like 90% of these derivatives: Citibank, Bank of America, HSBC, Wells Fargo, and J.P. Morgan Chase.]

even though they are insolvent - - while at the same time providing Government a hidden tax on the populace and access to unlimited debt (and unlimited spending).

Third, does it matter - if so, what to do? Of course it matters. We are paying dearly as the bubbles collapse, bringing down the entire economy. And the futile attempts to re-inflate the bubbles - - trillions of dollars that we don't even have in the first place - - are going to wreak further havoc down the road. They are asking us (no, *forcing* us) to reimburse the losses that the scammers and gamblers have incurred. "To save Main Street from even greater damage" . . . yeah, right.

What to do is the real question. Everyone is pointing fingers; each party is trying to conceal its own role, deny its responsibility. Because in the end it was a cartel of convenience and of mutual benefit: the banks benefited from Wall Street repackaging their waste; Wall Street benefited from the banks originating the stupid loans; the rating agencies benefited from Wall Street; politicians benefited because they were re-elected when the stupid loans were made; and the whole scam benefited when the politicians turned a blind eye, after all, getting re-elected seems to be the highest priority for a professional politician.

In the end, I think we are safe to say that our elected Senators and Representatives bear the ultimate responsibility. Spending recklessly; making unsustainable promises; incurring crippling debt; encouraging a false prosperity; and laying off the consequences on future generations. Legislating in violation of our "unalienable" rights. Denying the principles of sound economics. Ignoring the Constitution itself.

And allowing the giant banking Monopoly to continue, along with its immoral practice of fractional reserve banking. Not to mention requiring us to use fiat money.

On the one hand, it is sad to watch these poor souls in Congress as they hold their hearings and promise to "get to the bottom of this" and "act quickly to pass new regulations" that will "prevent" this from happening again. Really? When you do not even grasp the issues in the first place? When you are being misled, misdirected, and manipulated by the participants? And when you have put many of the perpetrators *in charge?*

On the other hand, as we economists say, it is hard to imagine that at least some of our Senators and Representatives don't know the truth. Maybe this is the way they *want* it. A Monopoly bank, controlling the quantity and value of money, has the ultimate control of the economy. Which means great wealth for the Banks, but at the same time grants enormous power to those in Government. At our expense.

Look – in the USA, it is Congress, and Congress alone, under our United States Constitution, which is allowed to make Federal laws and spend our money. Sure, the President can suggest and propose, strong-arm, even veto. But Congress holds the real cards; they legislate and they can override any veto. So which is it? Were our elected representatives simply uninformed and unaware, like we were? Are they now going to grasp what happened? (Were you able to understand what I explained, above? Will they?) And are they going to have the grit and honesty to take responsibility and to deal with the real systemic problems?

Or are they going to continue to pawn off these toxic assets on the taxpayers and on generations yet unborn, so that they can protect the systemic source of the poison, the banking Monopoly that spews out the worthless fiat paper money that we are forced, by law, to accept as legal tender, and by which, through Inflation, they seize our wealth. And our freedoms.

The scheme is unwinding. The confidence in the "confidence game" is shaken. The fact that our banks are insolvent cannot be concealed for much longer. And we must at last hold Congress accountable, lest we succumb to tyranny.

- - FPP - -

27. The Beach Boys (and girls): Endless Summer

Some of you don't drink alcohol. Maybe never did. But then some of us didn't bury ourselves in debt, either. But most of us have. Think about this little analogy:

It was summertime. The rowdy mobs of college kids were gathered at the beach; a few had apartments nearby, or RV's, but most just lived in tents or simply slept on the sand, when they slept at all. Each day was the same: when they finally woke and staggered to their feet in a stupor, shielding their eyes from the daylight, the first thing they wanted, the only thing they wanted, was for their throbbing headache to go away.

The cure was another drink. A Bloody Mary or a Tequila Sunrise. And sure enough, after a few drinks, the pain subsided. Then they started over, partied all day and well into the night, often until they were too drunk to stand. And while they partied, in their diminished, foggy state of mind, they were convinced that they were having the time of their life, that they were having enormous fun, that they were on top of the world. Not caring that they were not making any money or being productive. Not caring that they were living on credit cards after burning through every bit of their cash.

We know, of course, that the fun was mostly an illusion. That many hurt themselves. That foolish acts and irresponsible behavior became "normal". That fights, rape, and physical harm were part of the "fun". And that these kids were caught in a vicious circle, needlessly exposing themselves to addiction and self-destruction.

Of course the observers, the outsiders, the town folk nearby, saw what was happening; they knew the kids were not only hurting themselves, but were also damaging the beach and destroying property in town. But those kids, caught up in their endless summer, could see nothing wrong.

Look – I am not against drinking. And most of us have at one point or another gotten drunk or gone on a binge. And if not on alcohol, probably something else. In fact, that seems quite normal; if we never push the limits, how do we know where they are? But all parties, all summers, come to an end. And then what?

We Americans have been on a credit binge for the past 30 years. Cheap, inflated money was our high, like cheap alcohol at the beach. And we have, like alcoholics, become quite addicted to it. The only cure we seem to want, when the pain and hangovers arrive, is more. More credit. Which means more debt (they are two sides of the same coin). More spending. In fact, we are spending more than we produce. We are living on our credit cards; we have burned through our savings. We now fund our excesses with loans from China and Japan and other countries.

So the prosperous economy, the good times, the fun, were just an illusion. And Summer is over. The days are drawing short. The cold winds of Winter are approaching.

In the end, most of the college kids picked up and went home, returned to reality. And faced up to their real responsibilities, paid for their fling, finished school, and got jobs. But a few remain, to this day, alcoholics.

And now we Americans have to make the choice. Are we going to be hopelessly addicted, or are we going to face up to our responsibilities? Many of the observers, the outsiders, the folks in neighboring countries, can see the damage we are doing, not only to ourselves, but everywhere in the world. When they tell us so, we angrily argue that they are wrong and that *they* need to start spending more, too. (Spending money they do not have, racking up more debt, taking money from their citizens, like we do.) So that we can keep the Party going, make the Summer last all year.

Enough of the analogy. Analogies can only go so far. But it is a good one, don't you think?

I have a sense that the majority of Americans understand this concept. Most of us were against the bailouts and the TARP nonsense in the first place. But our fearless leaders forged ahead, they "had to act" - - fast - - and they rationalized ("rational lies") that they were doing it for our own good. Perhaps, they said, they were just not doing a good enough job of explaining to us how "necessary" it was, how important, how *good* of them to "invest" our money in failing businesses.

Are we going to face up to our debt addiction? Admit to our problem, face it, take responsibility, and pay the price for our mistakes? Go through the horrible pain of withdrawals (in the economy, those withdrawals are called a depression) and then prepare for a better future?

Or are we going to keep spending recklessly, trillions and trillions of dollars that we do not have, in effect force-feeding our kids and grandkids the same poison, making them addicts before they are even adults? Passing on to them the grand tradition of binges without consequences, and the lie of endless Summers?

- - FPP - -

Chapter 28. What in the world is an "economist"?

What is an economist? Do you know any? Work with one? Ever met a real economist?* That's a *profession*, yes? But when I look in the Yellow Pages, I find doctors and lawyers and accountants and all the other professionals - - but no heading called "economists".

Basically economists are people who study economics, the production, trade, and consumption of goods and services. The field started out as a social science, looking into individual behaviors and choices, and how those choices combine into an economy. And, as we have discussed, individual Rights, freely exercised, make up the trades that build a market economy.

Look at it this way: how many economic choices do you make in a typical day? Deciding which shampoo, which coffee, whether or not to eat breakfast. Choosing what clothes to wear, whether to stop at the store, what to have for lunch and dinner. Taking your break, or instead working through it. Perhaps taking the day off entirely. What to watch on TV, whether to rent a movie, whether to eat popcorn. Or dessert. Let alone the "yes" or "no" to requests from kids or family members. Everything we do has economic effects; I'll bet you could easily come up with at least thirty decisions that you make every day about whether, or not, or how, to spend money. (Probably more like a hundred.)

So at thirty a day, that's over 200 a week. Times 52 weeks is at least 10,000 per year. And do you always make the same decisions, or do many of them change from day-to-day? They change constantly, don't they? Based on different priorities in the ever-changing world around us.

Your choice about whether or not to buy that flavored coffee this morning affects the coffee store, which in turn affects the store owner's decisions, and so on; it ripples through the economy. Remember those free trade bricks that build an

[*footnote: Well, some of you may actually know an economist. Because I "am one" myself. I received my BBA in Economics some years back. While I have not practiced professionally, I have some strong feelings about my field and the way it is often "practiced".]

economy? Well, when you pile 10,000 of your "bricks", your economic decisions, into the economy each year, and when others do the same, it produces a very large castle indeed.

The population of America is now about 300 million people. Assuming a third of us are too young, or otherwise do not make economic decisions, figure 10,000 a year for two hundred million people; that's about 2,000 billion (two trillion) constantly-changing and evolving personal economic decisions each year. Each of which affects the economic decisions of everyone else, and together produce the "economy".

So here is the point: anyone who says they can control, or even predict, the results of all of those individual choices is either delusional or deceptive.

What *can* economists do? First and foremost, they can study the dynamics of choice, what people do, how that affects the larger market, and how resources are allocated. They can analyze trades and money and enterprise. These are really social studies versus "scientific" disciplines; these are the economics of individual Rights, "micro" economics.

And economists can calculate totals and identify trends, by compiling and analyzing data, which produces snapshots of the combined results of trillions of decisions. And this "macro" analysis can be very helpful in understanding what has happened economically, and in recognizing directions.

What economists *cannot* do: you have seen the movie where a van is parked outside, filled with hi-tech gear. Now picture economists as driving a big black van, studying their computer screens, headphones tuned to their listening devices. But this van has the front windows painted over. The economists can only look out the back window; they can see where they have been, but not where they are going. They could steer the van by watching out the back window, and that might work for a while; that is, until there is something in the road ahead, or until they come to a sharp curve or an intersection.

The problem in economics is not in identifying the trends, the problem comes when the economist tells us, or implies, that the trend will continue in the same direction, or indefinitely. Trends rarely extend in a straight line, nor do they go on forever. Remember the bagel craze a few years back? Bagel shops were going up everywhere. If that trend had continued, they would have outnumbered all other restaurants by now. Instead, it is hard to find one anymore; most of them disappeared almost as quickly as they came.

Or, think of a heavy rainstorm. And picture your weatherman saying, "If this continues, the entire city will be under fifty-four feet of water within eight months." Wait a minute, you would think, it never rains for eight months in a row, not even eight weeks; in fact, it rarely rains for eight days straight, what is he talking about?

Yet economists make those kinds of statements on a regular basis. Especially when it serves some ulterior motive to do so. While technically the statement may be true, its likelihood is so small as to make the overall premise false. (I read somewhere that the majority of professional economists work for Governments, and it makes you wonder if they might have a vested interest in making misleading statements that promote the goals of their employer, as job security.)

Economists make several other grave mistakes. Repeatedly. One is treating their field as if it were a physical science, as if they were studying electricity or gravity. Because while an electron or a dropped weight will respond the same each time, individuals may make different choices, may react entirely differently to the very same stimulus or opportunity (and often for reasons we cannot know). And it is those choices that make up the economy. Plain and simple, economics is not a physical science. And all of the "black box", computerized, hi-tech, high-brow, intellectualizing will not make it so. Nor the econometric models that are so prevalent in the field today.

Another common mistake - - actually more often a ploy - - is to use percentages rather than amounts (or vice-versa), resulting in distorted perceptions of the truth. Example: the economist says, "Sales were up over two hundred percent!" Wow. Must really be cooking, yes? But often they do not say whether that was this week over last, this quarter over the last quarter, or over the same period last year . . . And they may not provide the *amounts* from which the percentage is derived. In other words, if sales were only $100 last period and went up to $300 this period, maybe it's not a big deal at all. This perversion of data is rampant in what is reported to us as news.

A further distortion is achieved by comparing apples to oranges. "Diabetes is up xxx percent!" the headline reads. What they do not say is that the threshold for considering someone to have diabetes has been lowered, repeatedly, over the last few years; people who were considered borderline in the past - - and thus were not included - - are now counted as having the disease. The Government does this all the time with their "statistics" and data, for crime, for poverty, for inflation, for health, for cost-of-living, for GDP, and for virtually every issue where their economists compile numbers.

Finally, an issue which plagues many fields of study: determining cause and effect. Which came first, the chicken or the egg? Did "A" produce "B", or vice-versa? Or were both a result of something else entirely? In economics, it becomes especially troublesome when data is studied, in econometric models, as if it were a "science". When data streams move together, then statistical analysis is used to "prove" the cause-and-effect relationships. The flaw is that markets are made up of trillions of unscientific, sometimes emotional - - even illogical - - individual decisions. It is not a physical science. So all too often, the data streams that correlate are the result of entirely different causes, not one another. And in any event, the underlying individual decisions can change abruptly.

One example in economics is the theory of the "velocity of money". Simply put, it means that when money is moving around the economy quickly, then the economy is growing, booming. Makes sense. But when they then suggest that adding more money to the economy will increase the velocity, will heat up the economy, then that is non-sense. Money changes hands because people want to trade; when they do not want to trade, the flow of money slows; it's not the amount of money, but the desire for trade that makes the difference.

Lost American Principles: the Counter-revolution

As a (very generic) rule of thumb, when cause-and-effect relationships result from studies based in the social sciences, and the study of human nature, then they may have merit. But relationships whose validity is based on the output from black-box computer models that treat people like little, predictable electrons . . . well those are very likely to be wrong.

The old joke among economists is that it would be nice to find a one-armed economist, because they are always saying, "on the one hand" followed by, "on the other hand ".

So, economist that I am, here is what I would tell you: on the one hand we need economists to provide us with information and insight especially in the fields of individual choice, trade, money, and markets. *On the other hand*, one should not trust an economist who pretends to a "science" of economics; or, who implies that econometric models can predict the future (these computer models are in fact responsible for many of the derivatives and the "toxic assets" that plague us today; and, incredibly, the folks at the ratings agencies who used econometric models to produce AAA ratings on garbage still insist that they were "right"). Don't believe anyone who purports that the economy can be controlled from the top down, whether through controlling the interest rates, or the money supply, or intervention. Nor trust anyone who distorts numbers in order to create false perceptions.

In other words, we cannot trust most economists. And because numbers can be so manipulated as to "prove" what is false, in the end we must resort to our own common sense. And rely upon our Principles.

- - FPP - -

Chapter 29. Eat Your Vegetables

It was a small town, and isolated. Most of the moms insisted that their kids eat vegetables, because they were healthy. Only one farmer in the entire area, Johnson, grew broccoli, which was very popular. But he priced his product fairly, because he knew that if he overpriced it, one of two things would happen: (a) other farmers, seeing his high profit margins, would start growing broccoli, too, which would cut into his market share; or, (b) people would simply start buying peas or Brussels sprouts instead. Johnson had a monopoly on the broccoli market, but it was a tentative one; while he did not have competition, that could change at any time. And in the meantime, he was still providing win-win trades with his customers.

But then Johnson got greedy. First, he attempted to divert all the irrigation water for himself, leaving his competitors downstream without the means to grow their crops. While this violated their rights, had Johnson been able to continue for any length of time, the others would have been out of business. But the law stepped in and Johnson was ordered to stop the practice.

Johnson then tried another tactic. He got all the vegetable farmers together and they formed an association, the VFA. They all agreed to raise their prices, and they all began to enjoy increased profits. To the detriment of the consumers. And when the consumers began to complain about escalating vegetable costs, the VFA mounted a huge PR campaign suggesting that the only way to control these prices was for the town council to control the farmers, through a Vegetable Oversight Commission. The Commission was passed into law, with VFA people at the controls; after all, they were the experts. Thus the VFA, albeit indirectly, was permanently granted the Monopoly they had been seeking, now "legalized" and protected by the town Government. And from that time on, the town moms paid ever-higher prices in order to insure that their kids ate their veggies. The VFA cartel was able to avoid the price competition of free markets by operating under the umbrella of its Government-granted Monopoly, otherwise known as the Vegetable Oversight Commission. So what was supposedly created to protect the consumers wound up hurting them instead.

Another little fable that provides an important lesson in economics. Monopolies exist when there is only one seller/provider of a product or service. And is stronger when there are no close substitutes, or alternatives, for that product or service. But monopolies are not necessarily bad; they often develop in free markets because one entity provides the best value to the buyers and others simply cannot compete. As long as the Rights of both the consumers and the competitors are protected, which means that there are no artificial barriers to someone else coming along and doing a better job, then the fact that a monopoly has developed is of little concern.

Plus, monopolies eventually fail in free markets. Unless the freedom to compete is violated, new technologies, new ideas, new tools, new products, and changing tastes allow new players to come into the market, and they inevitably topple the monopolist.

But, little "m" monopolies can become big "M" Monopolies, which have many negative effects in an economy. A big "M" Monopoly has the two traits of every strong monopoly, single seller and no substitutes, but it also has one, or both, of these two attributes: (1) the Monopolist is allowed to violate the individual Rights of the people, in particular their Private Property Rights; and/or (2) Government uses its power to eliminate competition or set prices or otherwise "control" the marketplace. Either way, the Monopolist can operate without competition and without concern for providing win-win trades.

In other words, either Government does not guard against the Monopolist's violations of people's Rights; or, the Government itself violates individual Rights. Bottom line: a harmful, big "M" Monopoly can exist only with the permission of the Government; Government either shirks its duties or outright grants the Monopoly.

Examples are plentiful. In terms of Government shirking its duty to protect individual Rights, think of the robber barons of the past, who caused so many of the negative attitudes toward monopolies. Railroad magnates were allowed to trample people's Rights, to extort, threaten, mislead, seize, steal, injure and kill in order to build their "empires". Had those Rights been

Eat Your Vegetables

properly protected, had unfair business practices been halted, then these barons would not have been nearly as "successful"; they would have had to compete on a level playing field.

Same with the bankers. Had they not been allowed to practice the scheme of fractional reserves, an obvious violation of Private Property Rights, then they would not have enjoyed the windfall profits thus produced, nor would the "bank runs" have been so common.

It terms of the Government actually granting Monopolies, think again of the banks. The Government handed the bankers a Monopoly, similar to what Johnson and the vegetable farmers received, when they established the Federal Reserve. Then, on top of that, the Government did away with real money, replaced it with fiat paper, and granted the central bank the Monopoly on its production.

The Government has also allowed Monopoly powers in the health care industry; a few examples: physicians and their AMA; the drug company/FDA cartel; attorneys and their bar associations; and the insurance industry. Such Monopoly powers always violate individual Rights and the freedom to communicate, to choose and to trade, which in turn have negative and costly consequences whether in terms of your pocketbook or your liberty, usually both. Have you ever tried to get good information about the track records of doctors or attorneys? Do you wonder who controls how many students are admitted to law schools and medical schools? Do you question how insurance companies are able to sell policies and then make arbitrary decisions about how, and if, they pay legitimate claims? Are you amazed at the windfall payouts from class action lawsuits, and from seemingly frivolous suits? Are you concerned and frightened about the escalating cost of health care? Do you wonder why prescription drugs are so expensive in America? Why drug companies so influence doctors? Or why Americans use so many uncontrolled substances?

These Monopoly powers - - and many others - - when permitted by Government to trample our individual Rights, come at great cost and consequence to the people. Government often excuses itself by arguing that they are somehow "protecting" us, but the truth is that they are doing the opposite.

Lost American Principles: the Counter-revolution

      Government does have indispensable and invaluable roles to play in a free market: to ensure that individual Rights are guarded and protected, especially for those who are at a disadvantage or are a minority; to establish the rules for fair business practices and a level playing field; to referee; to set the example by using transparent, honest, fair accounting practices themselves; to provide for a real, honest system of money, refusing to Inflate the money supply; to be fiscally responsible and operate from balanced budgets; and to promote the principles of individual choice that bring about true and lasting prosperity.

      Government must not shirk its responsibilities. Government, in a free country, must not use force against the peoples' freedom to choose and must not grant Monopolies which do the same. Governments, in a free land, must not force moms to feed their kids vegetables. Nor grant Monopolies to those who would control the price and supply of vegetables.

- - FPP - -

Chapter 30. Going for the Gold

In 1913, the Federal Reserve was created. After a long propaganda campaign, Congress passed the bill, supposedly the solution to the problem of too much power in the hands of the bankers. Ironically, the actual legislation was crafted during a super-secret meeting of a few of the most powerful bankers of the day, including JP Morgan. Also present at that meeting was the Senator who then introduced their bill into Congress.

The Federal Reserve, the "Fed", is sort of a loose "partnership" between the US Government and the banking industry; the Fed itself is owned by member banks and other stockholders, but our Government appoints the Fed Governors. Establishing the Fed created a Monopoly banking cartel in the United States and provided the means to continue the practice of fractional reserve banking. Eventually, the Fed also became the Monopoly provider of the fiat currency that we are *required* to use in this country (because of the legal tender laws).

This central national bank would have been unthinkable to most of our Founders. And to many of our best thinkers. In fact, the Fifth Plank of the Communist Manifesto, the steps for moving a nation from capitalism to communism, is: "Centralization of credit in the hands of the State, by means of a national bank with State capital and an exclusive monopoly."

In 1913, we were still on the "gold standard"; that is, our coins were gold (and silver) and Notes could be exchanged for gold (or silver). That tended to anchor the value of our currency. At the same time, however, fractional reserve banking allowed Inflation of the money supply through vast extensions of credit and the bank's ability to create "money" out of thin air. Which led to bubbles. Which resulted in bursting bubbles.

In other words, Inflating the money supply distorted the markets and created the illusion of wealth and prosperity. But markets at some point demand a return to real values; as the bubbles unwind, deflation creates havoc in the economy. More credit, more of what created the problem in the first place, at best only prolongs the inevitable. And makes the pain and damage even worse when the accounting arrives.

Lost American Principles: the Counter-revolution

But during the credit bubbles in the 1920's, spurred on by the banks' new freedom to create money, we had not learned those lessons.* Rather than let the economy recover from its excesses, our Government employed bailouts and spending schemes on an unprecedented scale, in a vain attempt to prop up the house of cards. So we got the Great Depression.

Franklin D. Roosevelt then did the unthinkable. He signed a Presidential Order requiring all citizens to turn over their gold to the Government. (Oh yes, we were paid the "going rate" for our gold, but then he devalued the very money they paid us by about half!) This confiscation of our gold was clearly a violation of our private property Rights - - could it even have been Constitutional? Congress, however, quickly backed up FDR with legislation. So on top of the confiscation, the devaluation of our money further robbed us, while allowing Government to inflate-away much of its debt, at our expense.

So our own US Government took our gold, made it illegal to own. It was commonly thought at the time that the Government would return the gold once the crisis passed, but of course they did not. Which leads to the question: *Where did our gold go?*

Currently, the estimate of all of the gold ever mined, discovered and produced in the whole world is roughly 145,000 metric tons, or tonnes (about ten percent heavier than a US ton). By World War II, the United States held a large portion of the world's gold, at that time perhaps 20,000 tonnes. Today, our gold reserves are held in two vaults, one vault owned by the US Treasury at Fort Knox, and the other beneath the Federal Reserve Bank of New York. The United States is still considered

---

[*footnote: Today they tell us that they *have* learned the lessons from the Great Depression: they "learned" that in the 20's and 30's the Government simply did not bailout *fast* enough, or spend *enough* money, or create enough programs . . . so today, they are going to spend and spend, trillions and trillions of dollars, as quickly as possible . . . wow, they really know how to learn from history, yes?]

Going for the Gold

to hold the largest gold reserves in the world, but real numbers are hard to come by. You see, some countries will not reveal their gold reserves. Nor will the Federal Reserve, our own central bank. In fact, the Fed has never been completely audited. Never. In its whole 96-year history. It operates independently and secretly. That seems totally wrong, although there is currently a bill before Congress, HR 1207, with over 200 co-sponsors, that calls for an audit of the Federal Reserve.

So there is an estimated 4,500 tonnes or so of gold at Fort Knox - - we think, maybe - - and some 5,000 tonnes at the New York Fed. (Apparently we have lost about half of our gold reserves in the last sixty years.)

But if that's where our gold went, who really *owns* the gold in those two vaults? We might assume those reserves belong to all of us, indirectly, in the same we that we all "own" our National Parks. But - the Federal Reserve Bank of New York claims that it does not "own" the gold in its vaults. They say that they serve as "guardians" of that gold, which they "protect", at no charge, for the real owners: foreign nations, international organizations, and central banks (like the Fed itself?). But the Fed will not reveal who the owners are.

Furthermore, the Fed is now also the Monopoly provider of our fiat currency, the infamous Federal Reserve Note, which we are required, by law, to use and accept as our money. Today the Fed will no longer redeem those Notes for silver or gold. (Remember "Silver Certificates"? There was a time, not so long ago, when we had Notes that were redeemable for precious metals.)

But here's the irony: when the Fed loans money to the US Government, it requires those loans to be *backed by gold!* What a sweet deal: the bankers don't have to back their Federal Reserve Notes with gold, or with anything else; but, when our own United States Government borrows from them, the Fed requires those loans to be backed by Gold Certificates.

So it seems entirely possible that the Federal Reserve owns all of the United States' gold reserves - - either physically, or through their holdings of Gold Certificates. The Fed, the banking cartel owned by its private member banks and stockholders, may now own the gold that was taken from us.

If true, it means that our Government confiscated our gold and then traded it to the bankers in order finance out-of-control Government spending. We have paid the price - - as will our grandchildren - - by losing our gold in the first place, but also then by having our money constantly devalued. Private property has been taken from the people outright through confiscation, as well as secretly through the hidden tax of Inflation. And even more wealth has been transferred to the banks and bankers, not to mention the others who were in a position to benefit from the bubbles.*

If the bankers and the Fed do not own all of our gold, either outright or through Gold Certificates, then it is time for them to say so, and to disclose who does. Why is the Fed allowed to operate in nearly total secrecy in the first place?

The suggestion that we take our gold back deserves serious consideration. The premise is: we were *forced* to sell it to the Government, and the Government and the banks have profited handsomely from it. So now it is high time to force them to sell it back, paying them their official price of $42 per ounce. (Reparations?) And then use that gold to re-establish a real, honest system of money in the United States.

- - FPP - -

[*footnote: The practice of fractional reserve banking, as explained earlier, combined with a Monopoly on banking and money, has afforded these banks enormous, windfall profits over the last 90 years. Profits far in excess what of any "greedy oil company" or "capitalist" has received. Why has our Government allowed this to happen? Because Government also benefits when it can silently tax its citizens through Inflation, while at the same time gaining access to an unlimited source of spending and debt.]

Chapter 31. Real, Honest Money

Look – there is *nothing* better than gold for use as money. History has proven it. And fiat paper currencies have wreaked havoc throughout the world, along with the inevitable, intentional Inflation that follows. A growing number of people are starting to understand this. But too often they simply throw up their hands and say, "But we couldn't go back to a gold standard; it's too late. I just don't see how we could make the changeover."

And, of course, those who benefit from our Monopoly fiat money system - - and there are many folks, powerful folks, who benefit - - try to scare us and baffle us. "Gold is simply impractical in the modern world," they say, or "there's not enough gold" or any other number of it-can't-be-done proclamations. (Complexinators rational-lies.)

My Grandpa used to admonish me: every time I said the words, "I can't". He immediately responded, in no uncertain terms, "Can't never did anything." So let's take a look at how it *could* be done instead of focusing on all the reasons that it cannot. There are a lot of really bright, knowledgeable, creative, practical people out there who can make this work if we put our minds to it.

Assume that we pass a Constitutional Amendment that says: the American people have a *Right* - - an extension of their Private Property Rights - - to a sound, stable system of money; therefore:

(1) the Federal Reserve, the central national bank, will be phased out, eliminating the Monopoly and restoring competition in the banking industry;

(2) fractional reserves will be phased out and made illegal;

(3) the Federal Government will establish a standard for gold and silver coins (and for other precious metals as Congress shall deem appropriate) which will be recognized as money, to be minted by themselves and by the States, at each State's option;

Lost American Principles: the Counter-revolution

(4) coins so minted will not have a price or value affixed to them, but will contain a specified amount of precious metals;

(5) the exchange rate between coins of various metals will not be fixed;

(6) all Certificates and Notes issued by the Federal Government and/or the States shall be backed 100% by the physical precious metal that they represent, and freely exchangeable; and,

(7) the Federal Government shall recognize any coins minted to their standard, or Certificates and Notes issued against them, as legal payment for all debts public and private.

In other words, what if we re-adopted the gold standard? How we would do it? The physical part, minting gold and silver coins, is easy. Plus, the Federal Government can quickly replace our fiat paper Federal Reserve Notes with new Notes (in fact, they have geared up to replace all of our currency in a short period of time, in case of an emergency). They could produce US Government "G-notes", backed by and exchangeable for gold, in a range from 1/10 ounce to 1 ounce, plus larger Notes like 5 ounces and 10 ounces, whatever sizes we need. As well as "S-notes", backed by silver, for smaller transactions. (Or even "C-notes" of copper or "P-notes" of platinum if they were appropriate or necessary.)

The bills we use would be similar to what we use now, only they would represent a real commodity. And our coins would be like they used to be, as recently as about 4 decades ago - - made of real precious metals.

The positive results of this return to the gold standard are enormous. Ending the intentional Inflation of the money supply will take the boom and bust bubbles out of the economy (the normal, natural ebbs and flows of the economy will remain, but the credit bubbles, the false prosperities and the resulting firestorms will virtually disappear). A gold standard will also rob the Politicians of the ability to impose a hidden tax upon the populace, a tax which is not only very regressive in the first place, but also provides opportunity for even more transfer of wealth to the top. And the gold standard will take away Government access to unlimited spending.

The real question is: how will we make the transition? How do we get from a Monopoly fiat currency system and a national bank to a free banking system with honest money? And how can we do it with the least disruption?

It would not happen overnight, all at once. By transitioning over a period of years, we could have an interim "dual currency", our current Federal Reserve Notes plus, for example, five-year and ten-year Treasury Notes payable in gold. And with convertibility phased in over a time frame.

This return to the gold standard, to real, honest money, would restore fiscal confidence, rein in Inflation and deficit spending, and stabilize the economy. Moreover, when we experience productivity gains and prosperity, then more likely than not, they are real improvements and not just the illusions that evolve from bubbles.

This would also re-establish the reputation of the American dollar, which is in great jeopardy today. We have done the world a huge disservice by breeding, producing, and exporting our secretive, sinister system of central banks and fake money. And by not only living in excessive debt, but also encouraging them, forcing them, to follow suit. Real, honest money will provide the opportunity for us to redeem ourselves.

We know that the first major country to eliminate income taxes and establish a fair system (like the FairTax) will gain a huge competitive advantage in the worldwide marketplace. In the same way, the first major country to establish real, honest money will also gain an enormous advantage in growing itself out of our current economic problems, in building sustainable growth, and in ensuring the prosperity of its citizens.

- - FPP - -

Chapter 32. Guiding Principles of Economics

Here are some Guiding Principles of Economics, if the goals are freedom, peace, and prosperity:

1. Private Property Rights, along with the freedom to produce, to trade, and to profit (or fail) are the keys to economic growth. Even countries devoid of other liberties, communist China for example, have discovered this Principle, and have proven it.

2. Governments have no money except that which they first take from the people, by force if necessary. And that force must be used with great discretion. Taxing the citizens for any reason other than protecting and defending their individual Rights, results in violation of those Rights, and produces economic distortions which can only erode the causes of freedom, peace, and prosperity.

3. Inflation of the money supply is a hidden tax, an insidious tax, one that impacts most those who can least afford it. In a free land, Government has an obligation to ensure a real, honest system of money. And the only apparent solution is money backed by precious metals. Central banks, Monopolies, fiat money, legal tender laws, and fractional reserves are the hallmarks of Governments, and banking cartels, whose actions are in direct conflict with the interests and Rights of the citizens.

4. Credit is a curse, the siren song of false economies, when it is created out of thin air rather than from true capital formation, from savings. Credit and debt are two sides of the same coin. And the words can be interchanged. For every creditor, there has to be a debtor. To "get credit flowing" is the same as to "get debt increasing". And unless there is sufficient real capital set aside in the first place, it is a path to eventual destruction.

4. Because the Government's first responsibility is protecting and defending individual Rights, and because the Government

is also the ultimate defender of the Rule of Law (and the Constitution), then Government must maintain the highest level of fiscal Responsibility. If it would expect and enforce fiscal accountability for its citizens and businesses, then Government itself must practice the definitive standards of transparent and honest accounting. Government must spend as little of the people's money as possible; avoid debt; and, when temporary debt becomes unavoidable, pay off that debt as soon as possible.

No responsible Government would pass the debts of one generation on to future generations.

7. Governments cannot mix or "partner" with the voluntary sector, businesses and organizations, because Government brings *force,* rather than choice, into the marketplace, which limits the freedom to choose; distorts prices; and causes dysfunctional markets. The best the Government can do is to protect Individual choice and Private Property Rights; make and enforce the rules of fair play; and referee when costs are passed along to unwilling or unknowing parties (externalities).

8. Economies are made up of literally trillions of individual choices. All actions and decisions have economic effects; social choice and economic choice are also two sides of a coin. Thus, all attempts to control an economy "from the top down" will have negative consequences.

6. Prices are nothing more than the free speech of the markets, people communicating their willingness to trade, and their perceptions of win-win trades. Censoring, fixing, or otherwise interfering with this free speech warps the markets, with the same types of negative consequences as censoring the media and the press, which warps minds.

9. A monopoly, one provider of a product or service, often develops in free markets. And as long as Government defends individual Rights, a monopoly is not harmful, in and of itself, no matter the size. But Monopolies granted or allowed by Government under the law always disfigure the economy and trans-

Lost American Principles: the Counter-revolution

fer power, wealth, and freedom from the population at large to the privileged.

10. In a free land, where people take their responsibilities to heart, there will be "safety nets" for those in need, best provided voluntarily by churches and organizations and corporations. But if the Government finds it necessary to provide them, then they must not be "upside down". That is, they should be simple to obtain and immediately available for anyone in need, just for the asking; but safety nets should become harder and harder to stay in over time. Too many Government programs are very, very difficult, slow, and cumbersome to access, but once someone is in, they are "locked in" for the long haul - - that's backwards. As are programs that benefit most those whose needs are least, such as the Ponzi scheme that we call Social Security, which is falsely represented as a pension program of some sort, or an insurance policy.

- - FPP - -

Chapter 33. Democracy versus Capitalism

I bought a book called *The Money Men,* by H.W. Brands, * wanting to find out more about the history of the bankers and the forces that caused the creation of the central bank (the Fed). I was taken aback by a line in the Prologue: "The money question lay at the center of the *contest* between democracy and capitalism." [My italics.] The "contest"? What? It's one or the other? Mr. Brands, I thought to myself, has a warped sense of money and economics and democracy; and any book that starts with that premise cannot be very objective . . .

But then it struck me. That idea is very prevalent today, that capitalism and democracy are somehow at odds with one another, are mutually exclusive, are at war. In academia. In the media. In the literature. How sad, and how foolish. Because in a free country, democracy and capitalism must go together and must work together; they are "soul mates". And when they do not, we experience economic disruptions and loss of freedom.

We have talked about democracy, of, by and for the people, as the lifeblood of a free land. And we explained why it cannot work as the sole form of government, a big "D" Democracy, why it must be constrained by, and subject to, a Rule of Law. The same principle applies to capitalism.

Capitalism is nothing more than democracy at work, through a different channel than the voting booth. Capitalism is simply free people expressing their Private Property Rights. And voting with their dollars instead of with punch cards. Like democracy, capitalism must be subject to the Rule of Law. Private Property Rights need to be closely protected and guarded. And like democracy, if capitalism can operate over and above the Rule of Law, if it can violate individual Rights, then it becomes very dangerous, indeed. Dr. Thomas Sowell said, "Capitalism is not an 'ism.' It is closer to being the opposite of an 'ism,' because it is simply the freedom of ordinary people to make whatever economic transactions they can mutually agree to."

[*footnote: W.W. Norton & Company, Inc., 2006, page 16]

Folks often differentiate between their social lives and their economic lives. They say things like, "I believe in free markets, but I think it should be illegal for adults to smoke marijuana." Or, "I believe that what adults do in their own bedroom is nobody else's business, but I think the Government needs to regulate the money supply." What nonsense. That is the same as saying I believe people have individual rights in one aspect of their life, but not the other; that their left hand is free but not their right.

Can you think of a single activity that is without economic consequences? If you choose to be a vegetarian, for example, does that not affect what you spend money on? Or if you pursue a degree in music, where your education dollars go? If you make a speech, dance, or paint, does that not affect the things you buy? Doesn't your choice of religion affect how and where you spend your resources, and distribute your "stuff"? Wait, you say, "What if I choose to just stay home and not spend a dime?" Well, that probably affects your utility bills, maybe your cable TV package, and that choice obviously affects the larger economy, like the nearby restaurant that you stop visiting.

Every act each of us makes is also an economic act, so if we are free to act, then we are also free to make economic choices. Conversely, if our economic choices are controlled or limited, then our actions are controlled and limited.

Benjamin A. Rogge said, "Give me control over a man's economic actions, and hence over his means of survival, and except for a few occasional heroes, I'll promise to deliver to you men who think and write and behave as I want them to."

In a free country, there is no conflict, no "competition" between democracy and capitalism; both are protected, along with the individual Rights that produce them, under the Rule of Law.

"But, but, but . . . what about . . .? " (You are already thinking it, right?) "What about the Bernie Madoffs; what about recessions; what about monopolies, what about . . . ? Don't unchecked free markets wind up hurting people?"

Ah, but you answered your own questions. Because if our Government was about the business of protecting and defending individual Rights, then the markets would not be *allowed* to hurt people. The markets are nothing more than individuals exercising their freedom in the first place.

Those problems you enumerate, those issues, are invariably caused by Government *failing* to protect individual Rights. Or, by Government itself violating Rights with Monopolies and price controls and restrictions on the market.

We have already discussed how having a national bank, allowing fractional reserve banking, creating a Monopoly fiat money supply, and then Inflating it - - all Government actions, all in violation of individual Rights and free markets - - have made it possible for the Bernie Madoffs and many other scammers to even exist in the first place.

The wild economic swings are caused by those same mistakes. Sure, there would be undulations in the economy, naturally, but when the Government intervenes with attempts to "mess with nature", take the undulations out, keep things going up forever, then the inevitable corrections are going to be bigger, longer, wilder and more destructive.

We have talked about the difference between little "g" government and big "G" Government, between inflation and Inflation, between democracy and Democracy. What about capitalism? Yes, like the others, we can identify big "C" Capitalism; and, like the others it is dangerous and malicious. When capitalists are allowed to operate above the Rule of Law, when they are allowed to violate individual Rights, then Capitalism becomes nothing more than a variation of tyranny. How does that happen? Either by Government granting the Capitalists permission, or by "partnering" with them (think bankers, doctors, lawyers, farmers, and so on).

This has nothing to do with the *size* of the business, or "giant corporations", although unfortunately they are often the first to line up for special privileges. Why? Because the capitalist wants to gain an advantage in the marketplace; every capitalist does. But when they seek that advantage through Government, and its force, when they become Capitalists, they are

Lost American Principles: the Counter-revolution

receiving short-term personal gains at an incredible cost, for the free markets are damaged; individual Rights are breeched; the Idea of America is in put in peril; and our children and grandchildren will suffer the consequences. The capitalists are probably never going to stop asking the Government to make them Capitalists - - as we said, folks are flawed - - but our Representatives in Congress need to put aside their own short-term personal gains and have the grit to "just say no", to uphold their obligation to the people, by defending their Liberty.

Big "C" Capitalists, capitalists allowed to operate outside the Rule of Law, ignoring individual rights, are the bane of free enterprise systems; they do to capitalism/democracy what "kryptonite" does to Superman. Both kryptonite and Capitalists weaken - - and can destroy - - what are otherwise the strongest and most invincible forces in the world.

Am I saying we do not need regulations? That the market should be a free-for-all? Of course not! We need the Rule of Law in order to keep the markets free. We need to establish the rules of fair play and enforce them. We need Government to protect the markets from Capitalists. And from Monopolists. To referee. Because when ordinary individuals and traders and capitalists cannot participate freely, then the markets are no longer of, by, and for the people; the marketplace is no longer a democracy.

- - FPP - -

Chapter 34. The Great American Soap

Daytime "soap operas" have intrigued American television viewers for over thirty years. These shows have many dedicated fans, who eagerly await the outcome of the latest twist in the story.

While I cannot call myself a devotee, I have watched them occasionally over the years. It seems to me that the theme repeated most often is about someone who *pretends*, in order to accomplish some hidden agenda, often with a sinister motive.

For example: Sam wants Mary. But Mary is deeply in love with Fred. Fred makes Mary happy; Fred is all she ever wanted. So Sam pretends to be best friend, advisor, and helper to the couple, always there in a pinch. But at the first opportunity, Sam does two things: he persuades Fred that they must "partner" on the solution to some problem; and, he convinces Mary that Fred *needs* him in order to succeed, that he only has Mary's best interests at heart. And then, whether through sheer incompetence or mere manipulation, Sam causes the effort to fail. Mary is hurt and faces a dilemma.

So the trap is set. Sam tells Mary that Fred simply cannot make her happy, that he is the one that can do that . . .

The punch line is ironic: Mary turns to Sam, the very person who caused the problems in the first place. (It seems that Mary is the only one who cannot see that Fred is the only person that can truly make her truly happy. So the audience anxiously waits to see if she comes to her senses before it is too late.)

Sometimes the story revolves around a mother-in-law who does not like her son's choice of mate. Other times, it is not a relationship, but money or power that drives the plot. But the idea is simple: the manipulator pretends to be helping or befriending, all the while causing trouble and generating crisis. Yet the target inevitably turns to the manipulator, thinking that is the solution, when in fact the manipulator caused the dilemma in the first place, often intentionally. So the manipulator wins.

Lost American Principles: the Counter-revolution

America today is a giant soap opera, with many interacting stories. And many of them have this same plot. It might be black-comedy funny, were it not so sad and so true. Look at some of the story lines:

The economy. We have allowed the Government to put a chokehold on the free market by granting Monopoly powers to banks; by passing legal tender laws; and by Monopolizing our money. Plus we allowed them to Inflate the money supply and produce fiat money. The result is inflation and false booms and massive transfers of wealth, followed by severe recessions. So where do we turn? The Government. And their solution: more laws; more regulation of business; take over or "partner" with business; throttle the life out of free enterprise.

Health care. We have let the Government grant Monopoly-type powers to the medical and insurance industries, as well as the drug companies and their unholy alliance with the FDA. And we have asked the Government to feed our unquenchable thirst for revenge and monetary windfall via ludicrous lawsuits, with incredible punitive damages. Result? Out-of-control healthcare costs, putting a high percentage of Americans at the risk of not being able to receive even their basic needs. So where do we turn? To the Government. And their solution: nationalize our health care system. Let the Government do it.

Crime. We have made crimes out of things that are not crimes, prosecuting consenting adults who are hurting no one else, and as a consequence we have more of our citizens in prisons or on parole than any other country in the world. These laws have created huge black markets, resulting in even more crime, plus the loss of revenues and freedoms. Absurd "zero tolerance" laws have eliminated common sense and justice from the system. So where do we turn? To the Government. And their solution: more laws; tougher laws; escalate the "war" on crime.

So it goes, the American soap. Uncle Sam *wants* us, always has. As Thomas Jefferson said, "The natural progress of things is for liberty to yield and government to gain ground." But we were in love with our freedom. Freedom made us happy; freedom was all we ever wanted. So Uncle Sam pretended to be

The Great American Soap

best friend, advisor and helper to us and to our freedoms. But at the first opportunity, Sam did two things: he persuaded free markets and liberties that they needed to "partner" with him on some problem; and, he convinced us that was the only way freedom could succeed, that he only had our best interests at heart. And then, whether through sheer incompetence or mere manipulation, Sam caused the effort to fail. We were hurt. And facing a dilemma.

So the trap was set. Uncle Sam tells us that capitalism and individual Liberty simply cannot make us happy, cannot solve our problems, that only Government can do that . . .

How do you want this story to end? Do we turn to Uncle Sam, the very cause of the predicaments in the first place? Or are we going to come to our senses and realize that freedom is the only thing that will truly make us happy, before it is too late?

- - FPP - -

Chapter 35. Saved by the War

A commonly held belief is that World War II brought us out of the Great Depression. In fact, you can easily find books and articles about the "economic benefits" of many various wars. Professional historians are often the perpetrators of this nonsense, because they divide history into economic history and political history and military history; they ignore the reality that all of these are one and the same thing, each just different aspects, actions, and choices of the same society. The practitioners of the various "disciplines" even criticize one another, "What does *she* know about political history, she's an *economic* historian." It is absurd. And provides us with some very incomplete, sometimes terribly ignorant, history books.

When a person writes history from a purely political or social or war perspective, without a grounding in economic principles, or without taking them into account, they often come up with ludicrous conclusions, like "the war helped the economy." But, in fact, war can never help "the economy". Because, as we have explained, the economy is nothing more than people exercising their individual rights, making their own choices about their persons and their stuff. And war not only costs the citizens dearly in terms of their personal choices, but it also costs many of them their very lives.

Perhaps Jeannette Rankin said it best, "You can no more win a war than you can win an earthquake."

Look – if destroying buildings and blowing stuff up and killing people were so great for the economy, why wouldn't we just pick a US city each month and bomb it? We could keep the economy roaring. We could choose the city by lottery and give advance notice, allowing a short period of time for evacuation, to minimize the "collateral" damage. (But maybe given the severity of our current economic mess, we would have to bomb both New York and Los Angeles?)

Sure, we get "full employment" during a major war effort; the folks that are not dying on the battlefield are put to work at home supplying the warriors, caring for the wounded, or burying the dead. But vast amounts of resources are used to accomplish this, resources that could have been put to productive uses, rather than destructive. And how do we factor in the lives lost? What is each soldier, each son or daughter, each father or mother, worth?

On top of that, these wars are rarely funded. That is, countries do not pay for their wars from savings, from some store of cash. Nor are they able to tax the citizens, seize their property, at a high enough rate, to pay the expenses. So the Government goes into debt. And predictably, inevitably, they Inflate the money supply and devalue the money to pay off the war debts. Inflation is simply a tax, albeit a hidden one, and a tax that is very regressive, affecting the poor and middle class much more than those well off. So the cost of the war lingers for years and decades. The loss of our freedoms and the erosion of our economy over the last ninety years can be attributed in large part to our 20th century wars, and the fallout and bad decisions that followed.

Ernest Hemingway observed, "The first panacea for a mismanaged nation is inflation of the currency; the second is war. Both bring a temporary prosperity; both bring a permanent ruin. But both are the refuge of political and economic opportunists."

Of course, one can agree that sometimes war is necessary.
I would even argue for America to maintain the world's strongest, most-prepared, best-equipped military. For defense. Defense of our individual Right to Life. And the cost of maintaining that defense is one that most Americans are willing to bear. But if that military force is then used for nation-building, for insisting that other countries do things "our way", for meddling and playing other countries one against the other, then that is no different, economically, than blowing up one of our own cities. And no different morally than an "Aryan skinhead" killing a black man or a Jew.

Every four years, sometimes eight, we change our President and, at the same time, our "foreign policy". How are other countries supposed to deal with us? What if every other country changed its entire policy, and its attitude toward us, every four years?

Lost American Principles: the Counter-revolution

Why does Congress allow each new President to involve us in some new conflict, of the President's choosing? And why is our foreign policy in the hands of the President in the first place, rather than Congress?

Why do we maintain a US military presence in something like 130 countries around the world, about two-thirds of them? How would we feel about other countries, the Chinese for example, having bases in our country?

Somehow, step-by-step, rationalizing all the way ("rational lies"), over the last 90 years or so we have become the world's bully, the meddler, the know-it-all, the latest-greatest new empire. And then (some of us) wonder why we are mistrusted, looked down upon, and even hated by so many of our neighbors. Again, it is so ironic: often the people who most dislike the Federal folks meddling in their own personal lives are the very ones who would use that same Government to meddle with folks in other countries.

Edward L. Hudgins said, "Many of our fellow citizens no longer have the tolerant souls and morals of free men and women. They have the souls and morals of busybodies and petty tyrants who want to run their neighbors' lives."

And Reverend Jonathan Mayhew observed, "People are not usually deprived of their liberties all at once, but gradually, by one encroachment after another, as it is found they are disposed to bear them."

In short, war does immense damage to an economy, and the harm lasts for decades after the fighting stops. War costs the citizens of a country some of their individual freedom, as the Government "temporarily" violates their Rights, and assumes more power. Then, of course, the Government increases taxes, including the hidden tax of Inflation. And war violates - - rather than protects - - that most precious basic individual right, the Right to Life, as Government costs its citizens their lives.

Ah, but some are shouting, "That's not patriotic. If you don't like America, go somewhere else." Time to differentiate again. There is a huge difference between "nationalism" and "patriotism". A country gripped by nationalism, as was Nazi Germany for example, is very dangerous. When the mood be-

Saved by the War

comes "My country, right or wrong" - - that is nationalism - - then all too often it is wrong. And it gives the leaders the permission and the power to do whatever they wish.

Our American patriotic heroes were the ones who *questioned* their Government. Who wanted to be sure their country was on the right track. If one truly does love their country - - likes the Idea of America - - then wouldn't she want to be sure her Government was acting in ways that preserved and protected that Idea? Of course. And that means examining and questioning every Government action, keeping an "eye" on Government. Isn't that how democracy is supposed to work? So don't let the nationalist bullies shout you down when you are doing your patriotic duty. They are wrong, they are immoral, and they are dangerous if they believe that our Government can do no wrong. Especially when the overwhelming evidence is that their Government is so often wrong, in so many ways.

William Ellery Channing said, "The cry has been that when war is declared, all opposition should therefore be hushed. A sentiment more unworthy of a free country could hardly be propagated. If the doctrine be admitted, rulers have only to declare war and they are screened at once from scrutiny . . . In war, then, as in peace, assert the freedom of speech and of the press. Cling to this as the bulwark of all our rights and privileges."

Edwin Starr said in his song *War:*
"War, what is it good for? . . . absolutely nothin'."

There are times when a country fights a war in self-defense, of course, and then it can be said that the war serves a purpose, that it protects the individual Rights of its citizens. But starting a war, or provoking one, is another matter. Any "benefits", any "greater good" is far outweighed by the tragic and costly consequences, at least for a free country. I guess if you are a king or an emperor or a tyrant, and do not care about the costs and the consequences to others, then there may actually be gains that you consider "good". Good for you, anyway.

But is that what America is about?

War destroys lives and property and liberty. Any economic gains come at an immense cost, way beyond their value. Especially if the goals are freedom, peace, and prosperity. War should never be taken lightly; war should only be entered into as the last resort for defending our Rights; war should only be declared by Congress - - not the President - - as our Constitution demands; and war should have clear objectives and defined parameters for ending the fighting.

We can apply most of these same principles to our other American wars: the War on Crime; the War on Poverty; the War on Drugs; and the War on Terror, to name a few. They are entirely the wrong paradigm and have the same tragic costs and consequences. They are destroying lives and property and liberty, like every war does. And we have neither clear objectives nor parameters for ending these wars. Is it not time to have national objectives relating to peace and prosperity, rather than to eternal wars?

- - FPP - -

Chapter 36. Mirror, Mirror

Who is the fairest of them all? Do we really want the truth? It seems as though some Americans do not care to be objective, fearing for the security of their superiority complex.

There are any number of "freedom" tests and rankings out there, that purport to evaluate either the "economic freedom" of different countries; or, their "social freedoms" and violations of "human rights". But I have not yet located the one - - maybe it does exist - - that attempts to do both. Yet, our social actions impact and create our economic choices; they go hand-in-hand.

Nor have I seen a "test" that includes all of the Principles in this book, rating the protection and defense of all of our individual Rights and Liberties, as well as whether their accompanying Responsibilities are adequately met. For example: does the country ensure that all of its citizens have the basic requirements for survival: food, water, shelter and basic health care? Are those provided voluntarily or through force? Does the Government Inflate the money supply? Allow fractional reserve banking? Does the country have a simple, fair tax system? Does the Government practice transparency and follow generally accepted accounting rules? Does the country have laws which put consenting adults in jail for "infractions" which hurt no one but themselves? Does the country follow the Golden Rule in its relations with other countries?

Such a comprehensive test, based on the lost American Principles, might be very enlightening. In the meantime, perhaps we should take a long look in the mirror. Here are a few, certainly not all, of the telling observations we might make, if we would honestly assess ourselves:

Our Federal Government does not follow the same accounting standards that it insists upon for American businesses, and that most lower levels of Government use. For example, they show our current national debt at about $12 Trillion dollars, give or take, by using a "cash" accounting method. But if they were to use Generally Accepted Accounting Principles, like everyone else, they would have to include the (unfunded) liabilities such as Social Security and Medicare, and they would show our national debt at something like $70 Trillion dollars. Seventy Trillion. Or roughly half a million dollars of debt for each and every American family.

The numbers for inflation, cost-of-living, GDP, unemployment, and all the rest are manipulated and tinkered with until meaningful information and comparisons are impossible. The failure to use zero-based budgeting distorts the entire Federal appropriations process.

Our economy is in shambles. The Inflation-fueled bubbles are collapsing. The false economy is unwinding and reality is returning; the fiddler is demanding payment. Yet at a time when we are already up to our ears in debt, the Federal Government is not only pumping more of our money aimlessly into a doomed effort to revive the illusion of prosperity, but is also receiving far less tax revenues. Making the deficits even larger. And further increasing our national debt. It is ironic that one of the few sectors that is loaded with cash, that operates debt-free, and that is now making investments even in this down economy are the black marketers that we have put in business through prohibition. The drug cartels and organized criminals are buying up businesses at fire sale prices. And not only have we made them wealthy with our prohibitions, but their "earnings" are not taxed.

The US Tax Code is a monster. Like the plant in *Little Shop of Horrors,* it started out asking for a few drops of our blood, but now is eating us all alive. That we do not have the will to eliminate the IRS and the income tax, and replace it with the FairTax, speaks volumes about America's condition. As does that fact that we have nationalized and monopolized our banking system and unthinkingly accept scraps of nearly-worthless paper as our money.

We have the world's highest incarceration rate. According to Senator Jim Webb, "With 5% of the world's population, our country now houses nearly 25% of the world's reported prisoners. We currently incarcerate . . . [at] a rate nearly five times the average worldwide." Obviously something is wrong. Either we have the world's worst citizens; or, more likely, we are putting people in prisons for things that are not crimes and we have too many laws that attempt to control behaviors. Oh, and for a country that is supposed to be all about human rights, the percentage of black Americans, and other minorities, that are in our jails is a disgrace.

Americans may not wish for the USA to be an Empire, but in many respects, we walk the walk, and talk the talk, of Emperors. By maintaining an American military presence in two-thirds of the world's countries; by warring all over the globe; by attempting to coerce, change, and steer other countries; by both engaging in secret alliances and openly forming permanent ones; and by generally acting the part of a bully in many ways, we have alienated most of the world, which works against the American people. In fact, these actions often result in death for our own citizens. Andrew Kohut and Bruce Stokes wrote a book *America Against the World, How we are Different, and Why we are Disliked,* that shows the polls and the data.* We can debate *why* we are disliked, but to deny or pretend that we are not disliked, sometimes even hated, is simply refusing to accept reality.

And America has strayed a long way from the Ideas upon which it was founded. That we allow our own Constitution to be ignored and violated day in and day out by the Federal Government itself shows our inability to face up to the truth, to look in the mirror, to admit to our shortcomings and addictions, or to finally do something about them.

Look - America is full of good people. Like other countries. And we have an advantage in terms of freedom, peace, and prosperity: we had the Idea of America. We experimented and we found a formula that worked. We once enjoyed the benefits of following those Principles.

[*footnote: Times Books, Henry Holt and Company, LLC, 2006]

Lost American Principles: the Counter-revolution

Americans may have lost their way over the past 90 years, but we know where the right track lies. We know that democracy can work. And in our hearts, while most of us realize that we are adrift, we also still believe in those lost American Principles.

So it is within our power to re-affirm and strengthen our Constitution; to pass a second Bill of Rights; and to get America turned in the right direction again. *Simple*. All it takes is a total commitment to the goals; determination and grit; blood, sweat, and tears; a ton of really hard work; a healthy outlook; and a good sense of humor through it all. That may be a simplistic approach, but we are Americans; we can do it. You can see that in the mirror, too.

- - FPP - -

Chapter 37. Guiding Principles for Good Laws

The primary attribute of free societies is the recognition and protection of individual Rights via the Rule of Law. That is, the people in the society have agreed to be bound by laws that defend those Rights, and are thus assured their Liberty. This is most often accomplished through a Constitution, the Contract between the people and their Government, which becomes the law of the land.

But no amount of legislation or enforcement will be sufficient, short of absolute tyranny, to force people to go against their nature; to succumb to rules that violate their natural Rights; nor to obey laws that they do not respect. Bottom line -- in a free country -- the laws must be respected. And in order for people to respect the laws, *the laws must be respectable*.

Another way to say it is this: if free people choose, form, and control their Government ("of the people, by the people, and for the people"), then that Government would not pass laws that the people do not want, do not believe in, and do not respect. Otherwise the people are not free. Otherwise it is not a democracy.

Our elected representatives are so confused (or do they know exactly what they are doing?). They think that their job is to *legislate,* to pass more and more laws. When in fact, their primary responsibilities are: (a) to follow the law of the land, the Rule of Law, the Constitution; and (b) to protect and defend our Rights.

It is hard to see how what comes out of our Capitol these days does either of these things. Why do they go about endlessly passing new laws, never cleaning up or removing the old ones? Why do we have so many laws today that no one can even know them all, let alone understand them? I can think of at least two reasons. First, Job One for the professional politician is to get re-elected, no matter the cost. So if they can suggest or support some "new legislation" and then convince us that it benefits us, we will vote for them. And second, of course, the majority of them are attorneys, well-versed in the craft of producing vague and ambiguous laws - - and accustomed to profiting from them.

Consider these attributes of laws that are not respected: silly laws; unenforceable laws; unintelligible laws; too many laws; unpredictable laws; contradictory laws from different agencies; laws that may change on a whim; laws that are generic and have to be interpreted in Court, making compliance a matter of chance rather than choice; and, of course, laws that violate our inalienable Rights.

With each of these, not only do people ignore them, take their chances with being caught, but law enforcement folks often do not bother to enforce them, either, or do so randomly and arbitrarily. The people then begin to disrespect the police, as well as the laws.

So what makes for *respectable* laws? Here are some Guiding Principles, if the goals are freedom, peace, and prosperity:

1. Laws must be sufficiently few that the people can have knowledge of them.
2. Laws must be clear and understandable.
3. Laws must never violate individual Rights, nor the Constitution.
4. Laws must be durable; that is, in a reasonable time horizon, the law is not likely to change.
5. Laws must be enforceable. There must be some way to determine whether the law is being broken, without violating individual Rights.
6. Laws must be enforced. When the law is broken, the prescribed consequences must follow, without exceptions for the privileged.
7. Violations of the law are based on actions, not on thoughts.
8. Consequences are commensurate with the transgression. Restoration of victims is the first priority. While actions are the basis for determining violations, motive and state of mind are considered during sentencing.

9. And, any collection or body of laws can remain respectable only as long as the laws that are no longer needed, or do not follow these Principles, are updated or rescinded.

When we have bad laws, or too many laws, the entire system breaks down. Crime goes up. Enforcement becomes a huge problem. Jails fill up. So Government reacts with even more laws, often worse laws. (Stupid, knee-jerk reactions like "zero tolerance" and "three strikes".) And the whole system spirals ever downward.

America has become the land of legislators; look at how they judge one other: "What legislation did *you* get passed?" As a result we have more laws on the books than one could even imagine. Laws we don't even know about. Laws that even lawyers and courts cannot understand. Unfair and stupid laws. Laws that violate our liberties and the Constitution. Completely unenforceable laws. And because we have so many bad laws, many are simply ignored by the enforcers, as well. Every one of us is probably a "criminal", in violation of at least one law or another, perhaps without even knowing it.

For evidence we need to look no further than the IRS Code, the basis for our flawed income tax system. This may be the best example of the worst lawmaking the world has ever witnessed. It is neither understood nor understandable. The IRS Code, the tax laws, are so complicated and so perverse that neither the IRS itself nor the best accountants in world can understand it. No one can even agree on how large it is; here is what Representative Vito Fossella said, "the tax code runs 17,000 pages and contains a mind-boggling 5.5 million words. By way of comparison, *War and Peace* is only 1,444 pages and the Bible checks in at 1,291 pages." U.S. Representative Jim DeMint puts it at 44,000 pages; Representative Bobby Jindal says it is almost 60,000 pages. Whatever the actual size of the beast, it is, in a word: incomprehensible. And enforced, or enforceable? That's laughable. Only Americans' willingness to contribute their fair share, and their basic honesty, keeps the system stumbling along.

Un-respectable laws are not respected by the people. Why would they be? How can anyone expect it? When the people do not respect the law, they can only be made to follow it through the (extreme) application of deadly force. Only tyranny can enforce the massive tangle of laws that we are subject to; yet our elected representatives are hell-bent on piling more upon us. But then, that plays right into the hands of those that favor tyranny, whether they call it "socialism" or "communism" or whether they have some other subtle variation in mind. Will we be able to find and elect people who can start to undo the mess, rather than making it worse?

Or are we already too far down the road that Norman Thomas, six-time U.S. presidential candidate for the Socialist Party, predicted in 1944, when he said, "The American people will never knowingly adopt socialism. But under the name of 'liberalism' they will adopt every fragment of the socialist program until one day America will be a socialist nation without knowing how it happened . . . I no longer need to run as a Presidential candidate for the Socialist Party . . ."

Norman believed that the other mainstream Parties had already taken the road to socialism, under the banner of liberalism; and today, we seem to have a massive body of un-respectable laws, propagated by both Republicans and Democrats, that would prove him correct.

- - FPP - -

Chapter 38. Solar: the Energy of the Past

And other big-picture ideas. Concluding thoughts.

Sometimes we just get so involved in the details that we cannot pull back far enough to see the larger scale of things. The hard work is done, of course, at the detail level; still, it is important to detach occasionally, to look at the big, blue marble spinning through the universes; to try to open our minds to larger purposes; and to achieve some balance. Ponder these ideas:

Solar *is* the energy of the past. At the same time, solar is the energy of the future. In fact, the earth is just one giant solar collector; if the sun were to die, so would the earth. All life, all fuel, all energy comes either directly or indirectly from the sun. The "energy" question is simply how best to harness it, with the least long-term costs (which would include all of the costs).

What we call "land" and "countries" and "continents" are relatively thin layers of crust floating around on a core of molten liquid lava. The earth changes constantly as these plates move and collide and interact with the oceans. Earthquakes and volcanoes stir the pot. And the atmosphere is alive with electricity and winds and water. Weather cycles change. The whole marble goes from ice age to hot, and back again. Life forms spring into being and then disappear at incredible rates. In fact, the only constant is change.

The deep thinkers among us now tell us that ours is not the only solar system, nor even the only universe; in fact, they tell us, there are countless universes out there. Some say in a pattern.

So where do we fit into all of that? We are but identifiable specks in relation to the universes; yet we are a universe unto ourselves in terms of the atoms that make up our bodies. Why we are able to question our own purpose in the first place is a puzzle. That we have not only animal instincts and traits, but also emotions and reason and conscience is mysterious, indeed.

Lost American Principles: the Counter-revolution

It seems that each of us must come to our own conclusions of the meaning of it all, that no one else can do that for us.

Perhaps the best that we can do is to achieve some level of fulfillment and happiness while we are here, whatever that means to each of us. And allow others the same. Leave the world a bit better for our having been here. Perhaps help create an environment where our kids and grandkids can achieve even more fulfilling and happy lives. But do it in a way that does the same for our friends and fellow citizens; in fact, for everyone who inhabits the marble with us.

Killing one another; hating one another; using and abusing one another; or otherwise preventing our fellow humans from enjoying their chance at life seems contrary to any sense of cosmic justice or love or God. War, persecution, slavery, and death-dealing are the traits of a colony of killer ants without conscience; most of us aspire to a higher calling, a better purpose. And yet, what do you think was the leading cause of death in the Century just ended?

The leading cause of death in the 20th Century was not war. It was not cancer or heart failure. It was not a disease at all. More people died at the hands of their own Government than from any other cause. Dr. Rudolph J. Rummel puts the number at somewhere around 200 million, about six times more people than died in combat in all of the foreign and internal wars of the Century. Dr. Rummel calls it "democide", this death by Government, and includes in his numbers people who are killed by their own Government for reasons of race, religious beliefs, and political beliefs. Ought we to put all of our trust in the leading cause of death on the planet? (Government) Ah, but *our* Government is different . . .

At the end of the day, we must make decisions about how we want to live, day to day, interaction by interaction, relationship by relationship, and action by action. And we Americans enjoy a unique place in the history of our human race, one of the windows of time and place where we can actually choose the structure of our society rather than having it determined by a king or a tyrant or authoritarians. Choice. Freedom. Liberty. Rights. Wow, what an incredible opportunity!

But, of course, that means responsibility as well. If we do not learn, study, and understand our choices; if we do not defend our Freedoms; if we do not demand our Liberty; if we do not work at keeping our Rights, then they will evaporate, mere memories, a failed experiment. Because there are forces that would make our choices for us; there are would-be kings and tyrants, and swarms of authoritarians, who would prefer to tell us what to do. For our "own good".

In fact, these folks have revolted against the Idea of America and their revolution is in full swing. Could it be that we are people of history, the little group on the big, blue marble, that make their mark by putting down the revolution? By standing up to the seemingly overwhelming dark force of tyranny? By re-discovering the lost Principles? Can the Idea of America, of individual Freedom and Liberty, survive? Or will it be a flash in the pan, a falling star, an extinct idea? Will it disappear into a cosmic black hole?

We still have a choice. But the window of opportunity may be closing. Hopefully, you will be among those who rally, now, in order make a difference, so that we can accomplish the true changes in direction that are vital to saving the Idea of America.

Here is to a future which includes Freedom, Peace, and Prosperity. For all.

- - FPP - -

Appendix A. Constitutional Amendments

It is time to amend the Constitution. And to pass a "Second Bill of Rights". For these reasons: to re-affirm the Constitution; to close loopholes; and, to address some weaknesses. The Constitution was not perfect; the framers knew that, and said so. But they also provided the means to amend it. They never intended that it just be disregarded if a weakness became apparent, or when changing circumstances called for different solutions. Clearly, they would be appalled at the myriad of ways that the Rule of Law is ignored today, as well as the casual manner in which our elected officials violate the supreme law of the land.

How exactly is our Constitution violated? There are three general areas: (1) the Constitution is treated not as law, but as a set of guidelines; (2) some phrases, misinterpreted, have created loopholes; and, (3) Government officials act in ways that are outside the Constitution, or prohibited; all three branches of the Federal Government are guilty of this.

The Constitution is, and must be treated as, a Contract. It was by that agreement, that contract, that the States and the people created the national Government in the first place, detailed its structure, granted it certain powers, and specified what that Federal Government was - - and was not - - authorized to do. It is this Rule of Law, the supreme law of the land, which preserves freedom, constrains markets and democracy, and defends individual Rights. Treating this contract as a set of guidelines, calling it a "living" (changeable) document, and unilaterally deciding that it does not need to be followed will erode, and eventually destroy, our freedom. The Constitution needs to be re-affirmed. Amendments should specify that it is a legal, enforceable Contract. And the key ideas from the Declaration of Independence should also be repeated in the Constitution, as well as our lost American Principles.

Some of the loopholes are phrases, such as "promote the general Welfare" in the Preamble, which have been cited by the Federal Government as permission under the law to do all sorts of things that the States and the people never intended. The Feds could have as easily chosen the words "secure the Blessings of Liberty" to justify any number of illegal acts. These innocuous phrases were simply pointing out the long-term benefits of forming this new Government, not specifying its powers. The people knew that when they agreed to the Contract; everyone knew that. But the meanings of certain phrases have been intentionally twisted for the sole purpose of removing the restraints on power, restraints that the founders knew were necessary.

The basic assertion of a tyrant is that he has the right to control everything, every aspect of each person's life, if he chooses. Which is essentially the same right claimed by kings and communists and socialists. The silly distinctions by some, such as "we are socialist but not communist" rely upon the fact that they are willing to grant certain freedoms to the citizens. The problem is that these freedoms are viewed as permissions from the Government, not as unalienable Rights of the people.

So it is sad, today, that our own United States Government has come to the conclusion that it has the right to control everything, every aspect of each person's life, if it chooses. One phrase in our Contract, the "Commerce Clause" has been so stretched and distorted that it can be used to control virtually any personal act. As we have already seen, every act has economic consequences and thus this phrase can be, and has been, misinterpreted to give the Federal Government permission to control virtually any human activity.

"Necessary and Proper" has likewise been abused beyond the bounds of reason, or even common sense. These phrases were understood for what they were at the time the Contract was agreed to, but have been unilaterally and intentionally distorted. These phrases need clarification today, through Constitutional Amendment.

Another problematic "loophole" is the one of enforcement. If all three branches of the Republic violate our Contract - - they have and they do - - and if none of the three are willing or able to demand compliance, then how do the American people protect themselves? What recourse do we have? How do the

Lost American Principles: the Counter-revolution

States recover their rightful Constitutional powers? I have suggested a Fourth Branch of the Federal Government, the "States Branch" whose only power would be to veto or nullify un-Constitutional actions or legislation. (See page 62.) The framers had counted on the Senate to perform this function; but that was when Senators were appointed by the State legislatures and not by popular vote. We could either restore the State's selection of Senators; or, we could create a Fourth Branch with a much more specialized purpose. (Or perhaps there is an even better solution?) But somehow enforcement, and the consequences of violations of the Contract, must be addressed in the Second Bill of Rights.

And what are some of the weaknesses in the Constitution? There are many ideas to be considered at the Constitutional Convention. Here are some:

A balanced budget. Here is how I see it working: a two-year budget, rather than annual, to be passed in the summer of even-numbered (election) years. With the tax rate(s) simultaneously adjusted to fund, or balance, that budget. No exceptions for war, or for anything else; however, "deficits" and emergency spending are allowed, with the resulting tax rates set at a level sufficient to pay down a certain minimum percentage of the debt.

    Here is how it comes together: in the Spring of even-numbered years, Congress collects all the numbers from the Federal Government, income and expenses from all three branches. In the summer, they produce a budget for the next two years. Then, they adjust the tax rate so that it will fully fund that budget, including the pay-downs on the debt. The spending *and the resulting new tax rate* must be established, say, by the first day of September. Just a couple of months before the elections . . . !

    (By the way, the FairTax works beautifully in conjunction with this proposal.)

We have already talked about establishing a system of real, honest money; of the importance of eliminating the national

Appendix A: Constitutional Amendments

bank; making fractional reserves a crime; banning fiat currencies; and eliminating legal tender laws for anything other than real money. These elements need to be incorporated into one of the Amendments.

We should insist that our Federal Government comply with Generally Accepted Accounting Rules in all of their accounting and reporting (the same rules that American businesses are required to follow, and the rules that nearly all lower levels of Government use). This should include "zero-based" budgeting.

Elections have become a costly and time-consuming, all too often simply "Idol" type popularity contests. Some of that is to be expected; still, it is time to make some adjustments. Term limits: a maximum of three four-year terms in the House and two six-year terms in the Senate (a total of 24 years in Congress is enough for any one person); staggered 18-years terms for the Supreme Court (one new Justice every two years); and one six-year term for President.

Plus, it is time to eliminate the electoral college. Yes, there were valid reasons for setting up that system in the first place, in large part based on the lack of communications at the time. The main benefit was in representing the interests of less-populated States. But the cost of that benefit, the price we pay, is far too high. Because choosing our President by a *minority* vote of the people, often by just over 40%, is simply not right. (Just in recent years, Presidents Nixon, Clinton, and G. W. Bush were elected by a minority of the voters.) The electoral college has also guaranteed a two-party death grip on our political system by destroying the viability of third parties. So we need to make the change, elect our President by popular vote; and, when one candidate not receive at least 51% of the vote, hold a runoff election between the top two one month later.

We need to re-state that only Congress can make laws and spend our money, that the Executive and Legislative Branches cannot and must not. "Presidential Orders" and Court decisions, any actions by these two Branches, that have the effect of

Lost American Principles: the Counter-revolution

producing legislation or spending taxpayer dollars, without specific Congressional approval, must be halted.

And we should reiterate that only Congress may declare war. In fact, I would propose that Congress write a Statement of Foreign Policy every ten years, to which our entire Government is bound.

There are also some issues within our legal system that might be addressed at the Constitutional Convention. And a number of other good ideas. Like sunshine laws for all Federal legislation.

Look – most of these "Amendments" are not new; in fact most of these were the *intent* of both the founders and the States that accepted the new Contract originally. What has happened is that a revolution has taken place - - is happening right now - - a revolt against those original ideals and Principles. In order to put down the revolution, we are going to have to re-establish the Rule of Law. And the starting point is clarifying and validating the Constitution, reinforcing it as the supreme law of the land.

President Abraham Lincoln may have said it best, "This country, with its institutions, belongs to the people who inhabit it. Whenever they shall grow weary of the existing government, they can exercise their constitutional right of amending it . . ."

Well, I, for one, am not only weary, but wary of what our Government has become. It is time to exercise our Constitutional Right to effect these much-needed Amendments.

Appendix B: A new Political Party

Look – it is pretty clear that the two major Parties have a deathlock on politics. There may be a "left wing" and "right wing" in politics, but as someone said, today they are "two wings of the same bird". Most have become Republicrats, whose rhetoric is dramatically different, but whose actions are suspiciously similar. Neither Party represents me anymore. Many Americans feel that way, that they are without a Party. So I am suggesting a new Political Party:

The Volunteer Party
- - *FPP* - -
Freedom, Peace, and Prosperity
"that's all we ask of government"

I. Introduction

We believe in these <u>Fundamental Principles</u>:

We believe that:
- all people are created equal;
- all people have natural, unalienable Rights; and, that every Right defines corresponding Responsibilities;
- the most precious right is the Right to Life, the footing for the foundation of society;
- our Liberties, such as Freedom of Religion, complete that foundation;
- upon that foundation we can pursue our happiness, through Private Property Rights and personal Liberties, the freedoms to produce, to trade and to express ourselves.

We believe that the most basic, the most universal moral Principal is expressed in the Golden Rule: do unto others as you would have them do to you; never do to others what you do not want done to you.

We believe in the Principle of democracy for producing a Government of the people, by the people, and for the people - - a

Government, and a society, subject to the Rule of Law, through our Constitution. And that the primary responsibility of Government is to protect and defend the unalienable Rights of its citizens. In fact, there would be no other justification for the people to hand over some of their freedom, to grant Government the power to exercise deadly force against them, except to defend and protect their lives and their Rights.

We believe that from these Fundamental Principles we can derive Guiding Principles, not only for establishing Government, but also for deciding the tough issues that we will inevitably face. And for protecting ourselves when those who Govern are tempted to use their power to violate our Rights.

And, finally, we are not opposed to "big government". We believe that government should be *as big as it needs to be* in order to accomplish our goals: Freedom, Peace, and Prosperity. However: we define government as the people who make and enforce the rules for a given group, and we differentiate between the little "g" governments found in voluntary groups (clubs, organizations, churches, unions, partnerships, associations, foundations, corporations, etcetera) and the big "G" Governments that use deadly force to enforce their rules. We believe that voluntary efforts are more effective and less costly, in every case - - except our National defense - - and that the use of deadly force, via big "G" Governments, should only be used as a last resort, and even then only temporarily.

II. Preamble

Over the last ninety years or so, a revolution has quietly unfolded in America, a revolution against many, if not most, of the Fundamental Principles that we believe in. Look what ignoring those Principles has brought us: economic chaos; eternal wars; and loss of our freedoms. We are moving steadily away from freedom, peace, and prosperity; in fact, we find ourselves at the tipping point, on the brink of tyranny.

Appendix B: A new Political Party

As Johann W. Von Goethe said, "None are more hopelessly enslaved than those who falsely believe they are free."

The reason, and the need, for the Volunteer Party, then, is straightforward: to put down the revolution. To be the counter-revolutionaries who restore the Idea of America. We believe that this can still be done peacefully, through the democratic process. And by re-affirming and amending the Constitution.

And we who believe this way find ourselves without a Party.

The Republican and Democratic Parties have virtually abandoned any adherence to Principles; they have succumbed to the siren songs of politics and power, to the adrenaline rush of an all-powerful Government. They say they are different, but both Parties take us in the same direction.

The Democratic Party Platform, 2008, says, "Democrats . . . are reaching out today to Republicans, Independents and all Americans who hunger for a new direction." And the 2008 Republican Party Platform says, "we stand united today because we are the one party that speaks to all Americans - conservatives, moderates, libertarians, independents, and even liberals."

How can that be? How can *both* parties be for *everyone*? Simple, really: they do not adhere to any underlying Principles. They will be anything they need to be to get the votes.

The Democratic Platform goes on with fifty more pages of flowery rhetoric, with Government solutions to every imaginable problem. If any Government could really do all of these things, we would not be where we are today. They blame "the previous administration" for all of our ills. It says, "That is why today we come together, not *only* to prevent a Bush third term."

The Republican Platform is no better. Sure, you can find strategy differences. But in the end, it is still Government solutions to every issue. The Republicans have completely distorted the concept of "the rule of law". What that used to mean is a coun-

Lost American Principles: the Counter-revolution

try where we lived under the Rule of Law rather than the laws of rulers. But in their platform, the rule of law simply seems to mean passing more laws, placing ever more restrictions on our freedoms. They support a balanced budget *except in the case of war;* given that they promote and support endless and un-winnable wars, that rings very hollow.

Too many Libertarians go too far when they say that we should have no Government at all, that the Constitution is invalid, and that taxes are illegal. Especially when they promote anarchy.

The need for a new Party is apparent. For those who still believe in the Idea of America. For those who want a Government based upon those Principles, who desire a Government that is *bound* by those Principles.

III. Party Planks

We have only four party planks. Why only four? Because, unlike the other parties, we do not claim to have the answer to every conceivable problem. Instead of pretending that we do, and making promises that we could not possibly keep, we want to build a system, a framework, for finding solutions. If we have a foundation of principles, principles we all agree to, then we can engage in the healthy debates that lead to real results. We believe, as Thomas Freidman expounds in his book *The World is Flat*,* that the best ideas come from sharing ideas horizontally, not from top-down authoritarians.

Plank one. The income tax must be abolished. The best and most-viable alternative is the FairTax, now proposed in Congress.

Plank two. We must have a balanced Federal budget, with or without war. Our proposed amendment shows how that could be done, and still allow for emergency spending.

[*footnote: Picador / Farrar, Straus and Giroux, 2005, 2006, 2007]

Appendix B: A new Political Party

Plank three. We must dismantle the Monopoly central bank. Make fractional reserve banking illegal. And re-establish a system of real, sound money.

Plank four. We must re-affirm our Constitution, as part of the passage of a second Bill of Rights. And incorporate our Principles into the Constitution itself.

IV. Guiding Principles

Here, in our Party Platform, we would repeat the Guiding Principles for Government; for Economics; and for Good Laws, from Chapters 19, 32, and 37 of this book. (Pages 73, 121, and 140, respectively.)

V. Strategy

We know that at this time third Party candidates are at a huge, systemic disadvantage in national elections. (Local races are often a much different story; people have a real chance of being elected as Volunteers.)

The Volunteer Party would support candidates who run as Republicans or Democrats when that is their choice, if they pledge their support for the Principles of the Volunteer Party.

Who would do so? Republicans that can let go of their need to make crimes out of the personal choices of consenting adults that hurt no one else, as well as their inclinations to war abroad and engage in pre-emptive military actions. Democrats who can see the folly of debt and deficits and Government-run markets. And Libertarians who believe that anarchy is not a solution, that we still need Government, albeit limited.

Lost American Principles: the Counter-revolution

> ➤ So there you have it, a new political Party, the Volunteer Party. If you support the concept; if you want more information; if you want to join or to contribute, then please e-mail us at: theVolunteerParty@gmail.com

I encourage you to actually read the Party Platforms of the two Monopoly Parties:

The Democrats: www.democrats.org/a/party/platform.html

The Republicans: www.gopplatform2008.com

Chapter Notes and Resources

Unfortunately, many of the ideas and principles contained in this little book are foreign to many readers; certainly much of it is in stark contrast to what is considered "mainstream". I want to provide you a few sources for further exploration of topics that interest you, and perhaps for some confirmation of their validity. On the other hand (there goes my "economist" again), I do not want to overload you with a huge list that will be of no value; so I will attempt to keep the number of recommendations short.

If I were to have to choose just one book that everyone should read - - that's a tough choice - - it would have to be *Economics in One Lesson*, by Henry Hazlitt. [published by Three Rivers Press / Crown Publishers, Inc., 1946, 1962, 1979] Even though it was written forty years ago, the explanations are excellent and the principles are timeless. Americans are probably more illiterate about how economies work than they are on any other topic; this book can help correct that. It is short, non-technical, and easy to read.

Some people ask me, "But what can I do *now*, today?" It seems to me that two important bills in Congress are gaining momentum and could go a long way toward initiating our counter-revolution. The first is a bill in the House, HR 1207 that simply allows for a full audit of the central bank, the Federal Reserve (which operates in virtual secrecy and has never been audited). It currently has over 200 sponsors and could open the door to revamping our systems of banking and money. Watch the short videos at this site: www.campaignforliberty.com/campaigns/hr1207home.php

The second is the FairTax bill, HR 25 / S 296, which would abolish our system of income and payroll taxes. It's passage would declare to the world that the counter-revolution is for real, that we are serious about re-establishing the Idea of America. Please read one or both of these by Neal Boortz and John Linder: *The FairTax Book* [ReganBooks / HarperCollins, 2005] and *FairTax: the Truth* [HarperCollins, 2008]. Or visit the FairTax website at: www.fairtax.org And get behind the FairTax.

Lost American Principles: the Counter-revolution

Here are some notes and additional resources relevant to specific chapters in the book:

<u>Chapter Five</u>. (Einstein and Wayne) This chapter was included not for the purpose of changing anyone's mind about the Bible, or their beliefs; rather, it was intended to show that perfectly good people can have very different beliefs than what you or I do. And have a right to believe as they will, as long as they do not hurt anyone else.

Einstein and Wayne are not real, individual people; rather, they are a composite of many folks I have encountered over the years, both in Alaska and elsewhere. Wayne's opinions are likewise ideas that I have run across in a lifetime of reading and study; I cannot even begin to remember all of the "sources" . . . However, I recently read a fascinating book by David Plotz called *Good Book*, where some fresh perspectives on these ideas were presented; in any case, if you want some new insight into the Old Testament, I would certainly encourage you to read his book [HarperCollins, 2009]. Or google "David Plotz" for more info.

<u>Chapter One</u>. (Fundamental Principles) <u>The Golden Rule</u> has been adopted throughout history, and by many different cultures and religions; it is undoubtedly the most basic, most universal moral principle. For example, from ancient Greece:

- Thales: "Avoid doing what you would blame others for doing."

- Sextus: "What you wish your neighbors to be to you, such be also to them."

- Isocrates: "Do not do to others what would anger you if done to you by others."

- and Epictetus "What thou avoidest suffering thyself seek not to impose on others."

And from world-wide religions:

- Confucianiasm: ""Never impose on others what you would not choose for yourself."

Chapter Notes and Resources

- Buddhism: "One who, while himself seeking happiness, oppresses with violence other beings who also desire happiness, will not attain happiness hereafter."

- Islam: "Hurt no one so that no one may hurt you." Muhammad

- Christianity: "And as ye would that men should do to you, do ye also to them likewise."

<u>Chapter Fourteen</u>. (Four Dreams) Lysander Spooner was a philosopher who lived in the 1800's. He ideas are widely held by libertarians; or, more precisely, by the libertarians who believe in anarchy, who want no Government at all. Spooner, in my opinion, had some good concepts in regard to money and economics and freedom, but got crossed up when he tried to defend the concept of a society without the means to protect individual Rights. I think he did not differentiate between Rights and Responsibilities.

In any case, you can find more information by googling his name, or by going to: www.lysanderspooner.org

<u>Chapter Sixteen</u>. (is the Constitution perfect?) Alexander Hamilton was in favor a very powerful central government. In a letter to James Duane, in 1780, Hamilton wrote, "The confederation, in my opinion, should give congress a complete sovereignty . . . complete sovereignty in all that relates to war, peace, trade, finance; and to the management of foreign affairs; the right of declaring war, of raising armies . . . of equipping fleets . . . of building fortifications, arsenals, magazines . . . of making peace on such conditions as they think proper; of regulating trade, determining with what countries it shall be carried on; granting indulgences; laying prohibitions on all the articles of export or import; imposing duties, granting bounties and premiums for raising, exporting, or importing; and applying to their own use the product of these duties, only giving credit to the states on whom they are raised in the general account of revenues and expense; instituting admiralty courts . . . of coining money, establishing banks on such terms, and with such privileges, as they think proper; appropriating funds, and doing whatever else relates to the operations of finance; transacting everything with foreign nations; making alliances, offensive and defensive, treaties of commerce . . . the confederation should provide certain perpetual revenues, productive and easy of collection; a land tax, poll tax, or the like, which, together with the duties on

trade, and the unallocated lands, would give congress a substantial existence, and a stable foundation for their schemes of finance."

Hmmm. Those were Hamilton's authoritarian ideas for our new Government, although they were unpopular; and, that's *not* what wound up being agreed to in our Constitution. Yet that sounds eerily similar to the way the Federal Government conducts itself today . . .

Chapter Twenty-seven. (debt) For more information about the consequences and solutions to personal debt, pick up one of Michelle Singletary's books, or read her nationally-syndicated columns. She also had a website at: www.michellesingletary.com

For National Debt information, check out the "Debt Clock" at:
    www.brillig.com/debt_clock/

(note: this is the "cash" method of accounting for our national debt and does not include all of our unfunded liabilities, which would include Social Security and Medicare and would be about five times this amount)

Remember Ross Perot and his charts? He still maintains them and they are excellent. Go to: www.perotcharts.com   and click on "Charts"

Chapter Thirty. (confiscation of gold) The Federal Reserve, our central banking system (and not part of our Federal Government) has a shadowy beginning. Even though I am not much on conspiracy theories, the story is fascinating, if not frightening. While the Fed has operated with impunity, and in secrecy, since its inception; and while its nature and function is understood by few Americans, it is at last under some real public pressure. Just recently, the Chairman of the Federal Reserve broke tradition and gave a public interview while still serving in that position. And the Fed has also now hired a PR person, their own *lobbyist*, in what I feel is an effort to avert public scrutiny, or at least to "spin" their purposes and the effects of their actions.

For some perspectives on the Federal Reserve, try: www.youtube.com/watch?v=09NuAdKgqhI&annotation_id=annotation_341172&feature=iv

Chapter Notes and Resources

Or, visit: www.apfn.org/apfn/reserve2.htm

Chapter Thirty-one. (return to the gold standard) None other than the former Federal Reserve Chairman Alan Greenspan - - in his younger days a proponent of real, honest money - - commented on a return to the gold standard in 1981, according to the folks at gold-eagle.com. Read their article here: www.gold-eagle.com/greenspan011098.html

Chapter Thirty-six. (assessing ourselves) Senator Jim Webb has looked into the issue of too many Americans in prison. For more information on his hearings and his work, go to:
    www.webb.senate.gov/email/incarceration.html

He maintains a number of links there.

Chapter Thirty-eight. (big-picture ideas; concluding thoughts)
For information on "democide", the greatest cause of death in the 20th century, look into the work of Dr. Rudolph J. Rummel, professor emeritus of political science at the University of Hawaii:
    www.hawaii.edu/powerkills/20TH.HTM

Finally, you may wish to read any of P. J. O'Rourke's books, which convey their message through humor. Or the works of Dr. Thomas Sowell, if you like an intellectual approach. Plus, I especially like to read, and would recommend, the writings of Walter Williams and Larry Elder.

And you may want to subscribe to a free newsletter, sent via e-mail, from one of the skeptical observers of our American condition. While they will also include advertisements for their books and financial investment services, you do not have to buy anything, and their commentaries are invaluable. I especially like Bill Bonner's commentaries in the newsletter *The Daily Reckoning*.

Here is how they describe themselves: "Now in its 10th anniversary year, *The Daily Reckoning* is the flagship e-letter of Baltimore-based financial research firm and publishing group Agora Financial, a subsidiary of Agora Inc. *The Daily Reckoning* pro-

Lost American Principles: the Counter-revolution

vides over half a million subscribers with literary economic perspective, global market analysis, and contrarian investment ideas. Published daily in six countries and three languages, each issue delivers a feature-length article by a senior member of our team and a guest essay from one of many leading thinkers and nationally acclaimed columnists."

Just enter your e-mail address at www.dailyreckoning.com to sign up for free.

Glossary of Terms

capital is formed when people save, set money aside, rather than spending all of their income on consumption

capitalism occurs when people invest and risk capital, with the intention of increasing their prosperity; capitalism is a natural activity in a free society

Capitalism we define big "C" Capitalists as those who are allowed to violate the Rights of individuals, which is destructive to free markets

complexinators are those who argue that things are "too complex" nowadays, that simple truths and principles no longer apply

credit when someone is extended credit, they are able to borrow money and go into debt; credit and debt are two sides of the same coin and can be interchanged ("let's get credit flowing" is the same as saying "let's create more debt")

debt is the other side of the same transaction, when an offer to extend credit is accepted

Debt, National is the sum of our total liabilities; if our Federal Government used Generally Accepted Accounting Principles, our total National Debt would be about $70 trillion dollars, or roughly $500,000 for every American family. As it is, using their "cash" accounting method, they show our Debt at a "mere" $12 Trillion

deficit, National the deficit is just the amount that our Government spending exceeds its income in the current year. They are projecting nearly $2 Trillion this year alone; however, tax revenues may be significantly lower than projected in this current economic downturn, so the National deficit may be much higher this year. Our total domestic production, or GDP, is about $14 Trillion

democracy is a government of the people, by the people, and for the people, where the majority elects is leaders and representatives

Democracy big "D" Democracy is a Government where all laws are at the will of the people; majority vote is the supreme law of the land

Lost American Principles: the Counter-revolution

free trade is simply when people are free to trade something they own for something they want more

government in any given group of people, someone is responsible for making and enforcing the standards or rules; those responsible are the government of that group. Little "g" governments exist in groups where becoming, or remaining, a member of the group is *voluntary*

Government big "G" Governments exist when membership is not voluntary; when adherence to their rules is not voluntary; when the Government can confiscate its financial needs from the citizens; and when they can use deadly *force*

inflation the common usage means rising prices

Inflation an increase in the supply of money, which causes the value of the money to decrease and thus prices to increase. Prices, however, never increase evenly, or "across the board". Inflation has been used throughout history as a way to silently tax the populace; to transfer wealth from the bottom up; and to "inflate-away" excessive Government spending and debts

isolationist one who believes that we should not engage in military intervention in other countries *and* that there should be legal barriers to trade with other countries; that is, that the country should be an isolated island unto itself. An isolationist is very different from a non-interventionist, who believes that we should use our military only in self-defense, but still encourages free trade with other countries (this was George Washington's position)

liberal historically, this meant someone who believed in *liberty*, in free markets, in free trade, and in capitalism. The word has been twisted somehow, so that today it means the opposite, someone who does not believe in these, but generally still believes in the other personal liberties

magic of the market when two people voluntarily trade, they are both better off, because each now has something they wanted more

monopoly occurs when there is only one provider of a product or service in the marketplace, which is not necessarily a concern

Glossary of Terms

Monopoly a big "M" Monopoly is one where the Monopolist is allowed by Government to violate free markets and individual rights

nationalist one who believes "my country, right or wrong", that basically their Government can do no wrong. If someone questions or disagrees with Government actions, the nationalist will call them "unpatriotic" or say to them "if you don't like it here, leave". George Washington, and many others, have warned about the dangers of nationalism, which is the opposite of patriotism

non-interventionist one who believes that the military should be used only for defense of the lives of the citizens, not for *intervening* in the affairs of other countries. But that we should still engage in free trade with other countries

patriot one who believes that watching and questioning the actions of their Government is their right and their duty, that they have an obligation to oversee those who govern in order to defend freedom and liberty. Patriotism is the opposite of nationalism.

price is simply the language of free markets, people communicating the amounts for which they would trade

Price the big "P" Price is established after a trade has been made, the amounts that the traders settled upon

rational lies people often rationalize, but when they use unsound logic, untruths, or theories that violate Fundamental Principles in order to produce an argument that *sounds* logical, or rational, then we call their justifications "rational lies"

right something people are entitled to do, or have

Right a big "R" Right is a right that is recognized, protected, and defended under Rule of Law, a right that is not simply a temporary permission that can be taken away at the whim of Government

Rule of Law the Contract that establishes the Government, its Constitution, which becomes the supreme law of the land. That law supersedes the will of those who govern; it prevents abuses of individual Rights, majority votes not withstanding; and it constrains the tendencies of individuals, markets, and groups to profit at the expense of others

simplistic sometimes the truth is found in a simple principle. Those who disagree, or have conflicting objectives, often try to dismiss the proponents of a simple truth by calling them "simplistic", implying that they do not or cannot know what is "really happening". This condescension, employed by Complexinators, if unchallenged, often allows them to forge ahead with their agenda, neither defending their own position nor explaining why the simple principle is not true, or is not applicable

Index

AAA bonds, 98
Alexander Hamilton, 65
anarchists, 54, 55, 57
authoritarians, 33, 42, 54, 56, 57, 145, 154
bailout, 87-95, 114
balanced budget, 148
bankruptcy, 88, 89, 90, 93, 94
Banks, 81, 98, 100
"big government", 152
big "G" Governments, 35
big "M" Monopolies, 110
big "D" Democracy, 47
big "P" Price, 76
Capital, 85
Capitalism, 8, 85, 86, 123, 125, 160
Carl Marx, 23, 28
communists, 32, 52, 147
Constitution, 8, 3, 27, 34, 48, 53-66, 70, 73, 99, 121, 134, 137-141, 146, 148, 150, 152-158, 162
Constitutional Amendment, 147
consumption, 84
contracts, 58
debt, 1, 55, 70, 77, 83, 92, 98, 99, 101, 102, 103, 114, 116, 119, 120, 121, 131, 135, 136, 148, 156, 158, 160
demand deposits, 81
Democratic Party Platform, 153
econometric models, 97, 106, 107, 108
economist, 104
electoral college, 149
Empire, 51,52,55,57,63,95,132 137
FairTax, 119, 136, 149, 155

Federal Reserve, 80, 83, 98, 111, 113, 115, 116, 117, 118, 119
Federal Reserve Notes, 80
fourth branch, 62,148
fractional reserve, 81-83, 98, 99, 113, 116, 125, 135, 155
freedom of religion, 20
Free Trade, 75
Fundamental Principles, 1,7, 64, 151, 152
Gold Certificates, 115
gold standard, 113, 117, 118, 119
Golden Rule, 1, 4, 17, 29, 56, 69, 73, 135, 151
Great Depression, 114
Guiding Principles for Governments, 73
Guiding Principles of Economics, 120
Guiding Principles for Good Laws, 139
Idea of America, 1, 2, 57, 63, 66, 126, 133, 138, 145, 153, 154
incarceration rate, 137
Inflation, 77, 83, 92, 94, 99, 100, 113, 116, 117, 118, 119, 120, 125, 131, 132, 136, 160
IRS Code, 141
James Madison, 65
laws of rulers, 54, 73, 154
"liars loans", 96
little "d" democracy, 47
little "g" governments, 35
little "m" monopolies, 110
little "p" prices, 76
Magic of the Market, 76

Money, 78
new Political Party, 151
Presidential Orders, 150
Private Property Rights, 32, 59, 69, 70, 77, 110, 111, 117, 120, 121, 123, 151
professional Politicians, 49
Prosperity, 6,7
Ratings Agencies, 97
"rational lies", 48, 58, 92, 102, 132
Republican Platform, 154
Responsibilites, 67-72
rights, 21
Rule of Law, 27, 34, 53, 54, 55, 57, 60, 62, 66, 73, 121, 123, 124, 125, 126, 139, 146, 150, 152, 154, 162
run on the bank, 82

Savings, 84
second Bill of Rights, 138, 155
Self-defense, 4,30,131
sins, 44, 45
socialists, 32, 53, 54, 55, 57, 86, 147
Solar, 143
term limits, 149
the Volunteer Party, 151
Thomas Jefferson, 65
toxic assets, 89, 96- 98, 100, 108, 158
unalienable Rights, 48, 54, 63, 64, 66, 71, 147, 151, 152
velocity of money, 107
Volunteer Party, 151
War,130